SPEAKING OUT

SPEAKING OUT

THE NEW RULES OF BUSINESS LEADERSHIP COMMUNICATION

Matthew Kohut

Georgetown University Press / Washington, DC

The publisher is not responsible for third-party websites or their content. URL links were active at time of publication.

Library of Congress Cataloging-in-Publication Data

Names: Kohut, Matthew, author.
Title: Speaking out : the new rules of business leadership communication / Matthew Kohut.
Description: Washington, DC: Georgetown University Press, 2024. | Includes bibliographical references and index.
Identifiers: LCCN 2023052680 (print) | LCCN 2023052681 (ebook) | ISBN 9781647124731 (hardcover) | ISBN 9781647124748 (ebook)
Subjects: LCSH: Corporations—Public relations—United States. | Public relations—United States.| Business communication—United States. | Chief executive officers—United States. | Leadership.
Classification: LCC HD59.6.U6 K648 2024 (print) | LCC HD59.6.U6 (ebook) | DDC 659.2—dc23/eng/20240510
LC record available at https://lccn.loc.gov/2023052680
LC ebook record available at https://lccn.loc.gov/2023052681

∞ This paper meets the requirements of ANSI/NISO Z39.48-1992 (Permanence of Paper).

25 24   9 8 7 6 5 4 3 2 First printing
Printed in the United States of America

Cover design by Brad Norr
Interior design by Paul Hotvedt

There have been times when the public and the manufacturing industries have misunderstood each other; when the manufacturer assumed an antagonism on the part of the public which did not exist, and when the public took the position that the manufacturer was indifferent to the public welfare and solicitous only for his own prosperity. Such a situation should never have developed and would not have developed except for the lack of information of each party of the purpose and intent of the other.
—*Magnus W. Alexander, assistant to the president of General Electric, 1916*

CONTENTS

PREFACE

Gun violence. Voting rights. Abortion. Ukraine. These are just a few of the political and social issues that business leaders have addressed in recent years. This phenomenon has gone mainstream over the past decade, and it has changed expectations of executive communication. It has also sparked a backlash, particularly among politicians interested in stoking culture wars or defending industries that face challenges doing business as usual.

Corporate executives are increasingly under pressure from employees, customers, and others to see societal problems as business responsibilities.[1] Some see communicating about this as part of the job, while others resist it. There is good reason for concern about committing an unforced error by taking a position on an issue. But chief executive officers (CEOs) have always had to choose their words carefully when speaking to investors and markets. As technology has democratized flows of information, the more recent challenge is balancing the competing needs and interests of a wider range of stakeholders. *Speaking Out: The New Rules of Business Leadership Communication* explores why and how executives speak out, and it looks at the practices many have employed to meet the moment.

There are a few things this book is not. It is not meant to be a celebration of narcissism. While narcissism deserves consideration as a motivation for CEOs speaking out,[2] the focus here is on the broader trend of executives from a wide range of firms and sectors addressing political and social issues rather than on attention-starved edge cases such as Elon Musk. It is not intended to perpetuate a messianic view of corporate leaders as saviors or to glorify oversharers or abusers posing as altruists.[3]

This book is also not about the merits of investing or managing based on environmental, social, and governance (ESG) principles. ESG inevitably comes up since it has become a shorthand for any environmental, social, or political issue that a business might address, whether it is climate change or the rights of LGBTQ+ employees. This has led opponents of these efforts to weaponize the term "ESG" accordingly. Defenders of the fossil fuel industry focus primarily on the *E*, while culture warriors take aim at the *S*, but the objections all get lumped together. High-profile attacks on ESG and the CEOs who speak out are often, though not always, one and the same.

Speaking Out is also not a crisis communications handbook for navigating the shoals of political correctness or cancel culture. Adidas's decision to drop Kanye West in 2022 after his outburst of antisemitism was an example of crisis communications. West's reputation became an overnight liability to the brand, and Adidas cut him loose. Problem resolved.

Speaking out is something different. Scholars who have studied this type of communication have labeled it "CEO activism."[4] The term isn't new,[5] but in the current climate, it implies a liberal or progressive brand of action. (To my knowledge, no CEO has been called an activist for advocating for smaller federal budget deficits.) Yes, "shareholder activism" is also a term of art, but at the individual level, "activist" describes the shareholder, not the other way around. With CEOs, this is not always the case, as evidenced by a 2018 *Harvard Business Review* article titled "The New CEO Activists."[6]

That this moniker stuck is understandable because issues such as climate change once conjured images of tree-hugger brands such as Ben & Jerry's. But the label is problematic because it suggests a view of CEOs as liberals harboring personal agendas rather than pragmatists trying to deal with a dynamic world. It also doesn't square with the data. In 2020 two-thirds (68 percent) of S&P 1500 executives were Republicans, up five percentage points since 2008.[7] The reality is that corporations today in nearly every sector are expected to address issues that matter to a range of stakeholders, and business leaders often serve as the spokespeople for these messages.[8] Rather than characterizing this as activism, I'll simply refer to it throughout as "speaking out."

One challenge this presents is that CEOs must balance divergent interests in a country that's deeply divided along political, cultural, socioeconomic, and generational lines. They need to be utilitarian—maximizing benefit for a broad base of customers, employees, and shareholders—while also protecting the interests of the minority to ensure that those stakeholders can contribute to their companies as well.

Another challenge is that talk is cheap. Symbolic action serves a purpose in leadership, and some scholars characterize these activities as "strictly talk."[9] While it is tempting to dismiss anything a CEO says publicly as hot air, it's important to separate spin from substance. Protecting customers who encounter racism on a company's platform is not spin. Advocating for employees who lose access to medically necessary health care is not spin.

At the same time, scrutiny is essential. When the CEO of the parent company of Philip Morris USA proclaims, "We have an unprecedented opportunity to move beyond smoking," it's about as believable as BP's 2001 attempt to rebrand itself as "beyond petroleum."[10] An entity's size makes a difference when it comes to suspicion of pandering or putting lipstick on a pig. "The bigger you get, the harder you have to try to fight against the skepticism of your power," said Airbnb CEO Brian Chesky.[11]

While speaking out is commonly associated with CEOs, some companies choose to have the president, another C-level executive, or a senior vice president address specific issues.[12] Chief communications officers (or the equivalent) can serve as spokespeople, which can both deflect attention from the C-suite and diminish the significance of a statement.[13] The messenger makes a difference. Firms also have a continuum of choices about how and when to take a stance, ranging from live interviews or events to unattributed statements on corporate websites to joint communications with other businesses. When employees are the key stakeholders, leaders might communicate through an all-hands meeting or email. It is critical to get these tactical questions right, but the answers ultimately depend on the context.

The chief executives of publicly held corporations may appear alone in the spotlight, but notwithstanding rare exceptions such as Musk, they are typically surrounded by a phalanx of internal communication staffers, counsel, and outside consultants who advise, coach, and otherwise guard them from missteps. In smaller firms or those that are founder-led, these operations can be considerably more modest, and their CEOs often exercise a great deal more direct control over the entire communications function.

Having spent nearly twenty years helping leaders in the private, nonprofit, and public sectors prepare for media appearances and high-stakes speaking opportunities, I have observed up close how audience expectations have changed over time. As John Neffinger and I wrote a decade ago, "Orations are out—conversations are in."[14] Good leaders have always recognized the importance of understanding their audiences' concerns, interests, and emotions, but the need to be a listener as well as a speaker has never been higher. Where corporations are concerned, both employees and customers expect their voices to be heard. Technology, particularly social media, has played a huge part in reshaping that dynamic. Some of what has changed is substantive, and some of it is stylistic. This book deals primarily with the substance, though matters of style and authenticity come up in chapters 7 and 8, which consider the role of lived experience and values.

The focus here is primarily on American companies and business leaders. I draw on global survey data and point to some geographic differences, but most of the examples are based on social or political issues in the United States. At the same time, the leaders of multinational corporations know the importance of thinking geopolitically. Issues such as Russia's invasion of Ukraine in February 2022 demand that they think and speak globally as well as domestically, as do pressures from large foreign investors with different values and priorities than those of their American counterparts.

One of the risks in writing about this subject is that the landscape changes so rapidly. In mid-2021, for instance, CEOs grappled publicly with the question of COVID-19 vaccine mandates for their employees. Two years later, that concern faded from the headlines. It's safe to say that new issues will emerge that demand the attention of corporate leaders. The backlash detailed in chapter 4, which has already led some executives to proceed more cautiously in public,[15] will also continue to evolve, as will the counter-backlash that has pressured companies to stand up and take action.

And since this is an emergent field of study for academics, many questions remain unanswered, though scholarship is growing quickly. A quick search on Google Scholar for papers that address CEO activism returned five times as many results between 2019 and 2023 than between 2000 and 2018. A systematic literature review identified studies that have explored motivations for speaking out, stakeholder reactions to CEO statements, factors that can moderate the impact of a CEO's speaking out, and the effects that speaking out can have on perceptions of CEOs, their organizations, and the issues they address.[16] Current research runs the gamut from tightly focused experimental studies to broader analyses that consider topics ranging from stakeholder theory to corporate legitimacy.

With eyes wide open about this growing body of academic knowledge and the fleeting nature of hot topics, the focus of this book is on the dynamics that lead business executives to speak out as well as on the principles and practices that can inform and improve decisions about taking a stance. Just as it is still possible to learn lessons about effective crisis communications from Johnson & Johnson's response to the Tylenol tampering tragedy in 1982,[17] this book intends to provide an understanding of how executives effectively address political and social issues when necessary.

Chapter 1 defines the current landscape in which business leaders speak out on social and political issues. While CEOs became increasingly vocal during the 2010s, 2020 marked an inflection point: executives faced intense pressure to respond to extraordinary events. This trend has continued as challenges have emerged that called for clear, principled stands backed by action. Some CEOs publicly express disdain for this, but whether they like it or not, the current environment sometimes demands answers outside the boundaries of the boardroom, investor calls, and softball interviews on business TV channels.

Chapter 2 explores how we got here. Examples date back over half a century of executives from the biggest American firms taking stances on issues of importance to the public. Since then, battle lines have been drawn over the role of the private sector in serving the interests of shareholders versus those of stakeholders. The pendulum has swung back and forth, and the open question is whether action will match rhetoric over the long term.

The next chapter looks at the decline in public trust in institutions and the role that political partisanship has played in drawing business leaders into political and social issues. Partisanship has affected both the political views of executive teams and the appeal of brands to partisans on both sides of the divide in American politics. In recent years, CEOs have often spoken out in response to the failure of political leaders to protect their corporate stakeholders or to enact policies that promote long-term value.

Chapter 4 examines the political backlash that has taken root against ESG, diversity, equity, and inclusion (DEI) initiatives, so-called woke capitalism, and those CEOs who take stances on related issues. This counteraction started in states such as Florida, Texas, and West Virginia, and mushroomed across dozens of "red" states. It manifested as a battle waged against Larry Fink and BlackRock on multiple fronts, from state pension fund divestments to media attacks to a small, upstart asset management firm bankrolled by billionaires Peter Thiel and Bill Ackman. And it metastasized well beyond negative reactions to CEOs speaking out when social media activists drove boycotts of brands such as Bud Light and Target. The backlash also sparked a counter-backlash in "blue" states such as California and New York.

The fifth chapter starts by addressing the question of accountability and then offers brief case studies that illustrate four approaches companies take toward political and social issues: talking, doing, fence-sitting, and straddling. Examples include Microsoft's high degree of transparency on its diversity, equity, and inclusion efforts versus Wells Fargo's missteps; JPMorgan Chase's big commitment on racial justice; Disney's approach to addressing Florida's "Don't Say Gay" bill; corporate responses, including those of BP and Pfizer, to Russia's invasion of Ukraine; and Anheuser-Busch's handling of conservative activists' attack on Bud Light.

Chapters 6 through 10 spell out a set of principles and practices for business leaders as they navigate this terrain. Chapter 6 examines the importance of listening as leaders encounter complex social and political issues. Within firms, communication flows up as well as down, and intermediaries such as employee resource groups can help executives consider how best to combine words with action. They have myriad ways to tap into the voices of employees, customers, and investors, and executives who don't take the time to understand their stakeholders' perspectives and emotions do so at their peril.

Chapter 7 considers the importance of a leader's lived experience. CEOs such as Tim Cook of Apple and Kenneth Frazier (now retired) of Merck have drawn on their personal backgrounds to address social or political issues. Many leaders of purpose-driven businesses have a direct connection to their company's mission that can enable them to demonstrate shared concerns or interests with their customers or employees. Lived experience is not essential for speaking out, but it is a powerful source of credibility that positions a leader as more than an objective observer.

The next chapter looks at the importance of values. In a world where issues constantly arise and recede, values can serve as a guiding rubric for deciding when it's important to speak out. Corporate values statements may strike some as feel-good exercises, but they provide ballast when a firm needs to remind itself what matters. Speaking about values is often dismissed as virtue signaling, but virtue signaling is neither synonymous with left-leaning politics nor inherently cynical. Companies have engaged in it for decades; all that has changed in recent years is the political context.

Chapter 9 goes beyond values to action. It's one thing to say that Black lives matter or that climate change is the defining issue of our time, and it's another to act on it. Words without action erode the trust of employees, customers, and investors. Beyond the efforts of individual firms, networks that are dedicated to issues from racial equity to climate change can play an important role by holding firms accountable for walking the talk. Voluntary disclosures and audits offer other ways to build credibility for following through on commitments.

Chapter 10 emphasizes the importance of having a decision-making process to consider if, when, and how to address an issue. Speaking out doesn't provide political cover; it involves risk. An informed approach includes assessing the relevance of the issue, doing the stakeholder math, developing a game plan, and working through what-ifs and worst-case scenarios. Nobody hits the right notes all the time, and that knowledge only reinforces the importance of listening, remembering the importance of lived experience, navigating issues based on values, and backing words with actions.

Part I

THE NEW WORLD

1

A NEW PART OF THE JOB

BlackRock CEO Larry Fink's annual letter to CEOs in January 2020 was anything but ordinary. Most letters of this nature are the corporate equivalent of a State of the Union speech—a mix of business updates, MBA-speak, and cheerleading that attracts little attention. This one struck a decidedly different tone. Provocatively titled "A Fundamental Reshaping of Finance," it argued that the risks resulting from climate change were driving investors to "reassess core assumptions about modern finance."[1] A headline in the print edition of the *New York Times* captured the dramatic nature of this signal from the leader of the world's largest asset management firm: "New Lodestar for BlackRock: Climate Crisis."[2]

After underscoring BlackRock's responsibility as a fiduciary to its clients and stressing the promotion of long-term value, Fink laid out his core thesis: "Climate change has become a defining factor in companies' long-term prospects." He went on to list actions that BlackRock would begin to take, including "exiting investments that present a high sustainability-related risk, such as thermal coal producers," and "launching new investment products that screen fossil fuels." In other words, BlackRock would weigh the risks of climate change in its business decisions.

It didn't take long for the political supporters of the fossil fuel economy to interpret his letter as a declaration of war. They initiated a backlash against Fink and BlackRock that continues to this day, despite a string of decisions that made his 2020 position look increasingly rhetorical. (See chapter 4, "The Empire Strikes Back.") BlackRock quickly came in for criticism from climate advocates who accused the firm of talking a big game but not walking the walk.[3] Some said Fink's high-visibility swing hurt efforts to make progress on climate change.[4] And while today BlackRock maintains its lead as the world's largest investment firm in terms of total assets under management, it has been forced to dedicate significant time and money to managing the political fallout: in January 2023, Fink acknowledged that the backlash cost the firm $4 billion in assets under management in 2022.[5] (BlackRock took in $230 billion that year.)

Fink's 2020 letter was a far cry from the one he had penned in 2010 that made zero headlines for highlighting the importance of "combining efficient market exposures (beta) with opportunities to enhance returns (alpha)."[6] The difference in these letters illuminates a broader shift in business leadership communication that has unfolded over that decade and beyond.

Climate change is just one of a range of issues that top executives at companies large and small have addressed publicly in recent years. From marriage equality to the insurrection of January 6, 2020, CEOs find themselves confronted with a constantly changing slate of political and social issues that affect their employees, investors, suppliers, and customers. While the heads of S&P 500 companies generate the most attention when speaking out, leaders of smaller businesses and start-up founders also face this landscape, and they have different constituencies and considerations than their peers in publicly traded companies.

This represents a sweeping change from the era in which most of today's chief executives joined the workforce; previously, corporate leaders generally tried to avoid political and social hot buttons at all costs. The late-twentieth-century paradigm for corporate communication about social issues was captured (and ridiculed) by Michael Moore in his 1989 film *Roger & Me*, which featured Moore doggedly trying to engage General Motors (GM) CEO Roger Smith in a dialogue about Flint, Michigan, a town that fell on desperate times after GM laid off thousands of employees who lived there. Smith evaded Moore whenever he could and obfuscated when Moore finally confronted him at a shareholder meeting. In this same period, Chrysler, among other companies, pulled its advertising from Ellen DeGeneres's sitcom *Ellen* after her character, Ellen, came out as gay on the show. "We don't think it is a smart business decision to be advertising in an environment that is so polarized," a spokeswoman for Chrysler said at the time.[7]

Chief executives can no longer avoid divisive political and social topics, even if they sometimes would prefer to. "This is an issue that's facing every CEO in the world right now," said Nike CEO John Donahoe when he took the top job at the company in early 2020.[8]

It's impossible to identify a single moment when this shift took root. In 2016 Bank of America CEO Brian Moynihan observed, "Our jobs as CEOs now include driving what we think is right," which he defined as "action on issues beyond business."[9] By that time, Moynihan was simply articulating an unwritten part of the job description that he and his peers had been doing for years. Consider the following examples:

2013: Starbucks CEO Howard Schultz writes an open letter titled "Our Respectful Request" asking gun owners not to bring their weapons into stores in states with open carry laws.[10]

2012: Chick-fil-A CEO Dan Cathy makes a religious argument in opposition to marriage equality for lesbian, gay, bisexual, transgender, queer, and other (LGBTQ+) people.[11]

2010: General Electric CEO Jeffrey Immelt describes US energy policy as "just stupid," noting that the rest of the world is moving "10 times faster" toward renewable energy.[12]

2009: Whole Foods CEO John Mackey writes an op-ed in the *Wall Street Journal* proposing health care reforms that follow the Whole Foods' approach to health benefits rather than the proposed program under the Affordable Care Act, or Obamacare.[13]

The slippery part of Moynihan's formulation is that "what we think is right" meant something different to each of these leaders. On divisive cultural issues, both Schultz and Cathy likely won favor with some customers and alienated others. Determining if that helped or hurt from a business standpoint boils down to knowing the customer math. (See chapter 10, "Have a Process.") Immelt and Mackey each criticized policymakers, a move that probably had little impact for their companies at the time, but as chapter 4 details, that is not always the case today.

If speaking out went mainstream in the 2010s, 2020 marked a turning point when it reached critical mass. Larry Fink's letter in January was big news in the investor and business communities, but the events that followed touched every level of society. A few weeks later, the COVID-19 pandemic swept the globe, forcing millions out of jobs and millions more into remote work overnight. The murder of George Floyd by a Minneapolis police officer in May pressured corporate leaders to confront grievous systemic injustices. Sitting on the sidelines came with a cost.

The outrage over George Floyd's death marked a noticeable spike in public engagement by business leaders,[14] but it was not an isolated event. Since then, hundreds of CEOs have weighed in on issues from voting rights to gun violence prevention to Russia's invasion of Ukraine. A 2022 Conference Board survey of three hundred public, private, and nonprofit organizations found that racial equality (61 percent) and LGBTQ+ rights (44 percent) were the social issues most commonly addressed in public statements over the previous two years, followed by COVID-related topics (40 percent) and gender equality (39 percent).[15] "Stating the obvious, companies are now asked to participate in a much wider set of issues," said Michael Dell, founder, chairman, and CEO of Dell Technologies.[16]

Is It Legitimate for CEOs to Speak Out?

Critics blast all of this as the capitulation of corporate America to so-called woke politics. Former Roivant Sciences CEO Vivek Ramaswamy, perhaps the best-known advocate for this point of view, published a full-length polemic on the topic. (See chapter 4.) One of his arguments is that corporations don't belong in politics, period. "This new model of capitalism demands a dangerous expansion of corporate power that threatens to subvert American democracy," he wrote.[17]

Ramaswamy is not alone in staking out a position along these lines. In 2021, Senate minority leader Mitch McConnell warned, "From election law to environmentalism to radical social agendas to the Second Amendment, parts of the private sector keep dabbling in behaving like a woke parallel government."[18]

Important concerns about the balance of power between the private and public sectors are beyond the scope of this book. Apple currently tops $3 trillion in market cap,[19] and its activities extend well beyond technology to banking and news aggregation. After Russia invaded

Ukraine, privately owned SpaceX provided internet access to war-torn Ukraine through its Starlink system, giving Elon Musk the power to turn off its internet service at will.[20] Putting aside the broader questions about the growing concentration of corporate power raised by such cases, the relationship between business and government in the United States is more complicated than Ramaswamy or McConnell let on.

First, corporations have made their voices heard in politics for decades. Through trade associations, hard money, soft money, and dark money, businesses have any number of ways in the post–*Citizens United* landscape to flex their political muscle. McConnell's protest about corporate involvement in Second Amendment politics was highly selective. In the same year that he leveled this charge, the National Shooting Sports Foundation, whose board of governors includes executives from Smith & Wesson, Beretta, Glock, Browning Arms, and Sturm, Ruger & Co., spent $5 million on federal lobbying activities.[21] McConnell's accusation boils down to a preference for some corporations dabbling in politics rather than others.

What has changed is that CEOs' voices are now in the mix, sometimes in opposition to other corporate interests (such as those represented by the National Shooting Sports Foundation). From a standpoint of democratic legitimacy, it seems better for a bank to state publicly why it chooses not to process transactions for businesses that sell military-style assault weapons than for the manufacturers of those weapons to pull political strings out of public view.[22]

Second, for many corporations, strategy is inseparable from politics for reasons having nothing to do with partisanship. Divestment from Russia does not fall neatly on one side of the political spectrum. Climate change is inherently a corporate problem: a hundred firms were responsible for 70 percent of greenhouse gas emissions between 1988 and 2015, and a significant number of those corporations are investor owned.[23] Laws that promote discrimination or restrict individual rights can prompt CEOs to look for ways to protect their employees, and that can set CEOs in opposition to powerful political leaders at the state or federal level. These challenging questions can't be sidestepped. "The strategic context of business is the CEO's lane," wrote Jeffrey Sonnenfeld of Yale University's Chief Executive Leadership Institute in the *Economist*.[24]

Where speaking out is concerned, transparency and accountability are the twin pillars of legitimacy. In some cases, corporations can employ established practices such as independent audits and voluntary disclosures that confer legitimacy on their words and actions.[25] These actions have become increasingly common with issues such as climate change and diversity, equity, and inclusion (DEI). (See chapter 9, "Values Are Not Enough.")

Why the CEO?

The need for business leaders to speak publicly on behalf of the organization has always been part of the job description. In 1973, Henry Mintzberg identified "spokesman [sic]" as one of ten managerial roles, noting that the duties included the responsibility for talking to "suppliers, trade organizations, peers, government agencies, customers, and the press."[26] Today, most firms (62 percent) rely on top executives to communicate with the public, though this differs across geographic and cultural boundaries. It is a far more common approach for companies headquartered in the United States and Europe than for those based in Japan or China.[27]

What has changed is the extent to which CEOs now speak out directly on political and social issues rather than operating exclusively behind the scenes or through intermediaries such as trade associations or lobbyists.[28] The internet, and social media in particular, has also exploded the speed at which every utterance goes instantly global.

At this point, surveys show strong support globally for CEOs speaking out. The 2022 Edelman Trust Barometer found that eight in ten (81 percent) surveyed in twenty-seven countries agreed that CEOs should be personally visible when discussing public policy with external stakeholders or the work their company has done to benefit society.[29] Publics in fourteen countries expect that CEOs will inform policy debates on social issues including wage inequality (72 percent), global warming and climate change (71 percent), and prejudice and discrimination (68 percent).[30]

As of this writing, most Americans expect CEOs to take stances on political and social issues, but they have differing views about when CEOs should weigh in. A plurality (42 percent) says chief executives should only

Where speaking out is concerned, transparency and accountability are the twin pillars of legitimacy.

make statements about or get involved in issues directly related to their business, while one in four (27 percent) think they should get involved in general.[31] But there are strong generational differences. Members of Generation Z (Gen Zers) are twice as likely as baby boomers to say CEOs should generally get involved (40 percent versus 20 percent).

Public support for CEOs' speaking out has been steady for several years. From 2018 to 2021, solid majorities of Americans said CEOs should take a stand on important societal issues.[32] This is consistent with the public's views on the broader role of business in society: more than three out of four people believe business can be a powerful force of societal change (81 percent) and that companies have a responsibility to behave like a good citizen and to consider their impacts on other people and the planet (77 percent).[33] But these aggregate findings tell an incomplete story because views on corporate positions on issues are highly influenced by partisanship. (See chapter 3, "Filling the Void.")

Since the ability to engage on a wide range of issues has become a more important part of the job, companies increasingly look for outstanding communication and social skills when hiring new CEOs. A study of five thousand C-suite job descriptions from 2000 to 2017 revealed that companies now seek leaders who can communicate "personally and transparently and accountably."[34] This marks a significant departure from a generation ago, when job descriptions emphasized "hard" management skills that are more easily measured. The importance of transparency and accountability cannot be overstated. As former Starbucks CEO Howard Schultz put it, "In the world we're living in, no company, no CEO can hide. Everyone knows everything. Everything you say publicly or privately is out there."[35]

Why Do CEOs Speak Out?

There's not a single reason. At the most fundamental level, CEOs are either trying to influence stakeholders or using their platforms to express their personal views.[36] But a few more specific plausible explanations inevitably overlap.

Sometimes CEOs want to explain business decisions that touch on sociopolitical issues. When Airbnb kicked off the platform a million people who refused to check a box saying they wouldn't discriminate against people, it did so to address complaints of racism from Black users. "This platform is not going to work if people aren't going to accept one another from different values," said CEO Brian Chesky.[37] Similarly, when airline CEOs spoke out about vaccines for employees in 2021, they weren't explicitly trying to make political statements; rather, they found themselves dealing with a health and safety issue that had been politicized.[38]

In other instances, CEOs explicitly address issues that matter to their employees or customers. In some cases, they respond to an issue that directly affects many people (e.g., access to abortion for employees), while other times they express support for something that people feel strongly about, such as outrage about mass shootings. Where employees are concerned, it's important to recognize that this communication often happens internally rather than through public statements. "I have 6800 employees. They're what I'm focused on," said Dana Maiman, CEO of IPG Health.[39]

CEOs also use their platform to do what they think is right for society, even when the connection to their businesses may appear indirect. Levi Strauss CEO Chip Bergh made the case for helping employees exercise their right to vote. "We try to be non-partisan and non-political on this. But we are one of the only true democracies where elections happen on a workday," he said.[40]

In some cases, CEOs use their platforms to address personal priorities connected to social issues. For example, some executives have spoken candidly about their own mental health challenges to help destigmatize the issue. (See chapter 7, "Lived Experience Matters.") This is not substantively different from supporting efforts to eradicate cancer or to save the environment, but the latter are unlikely to draw much public attention because they are more familiar and less taboo. The line between advancing a personal priority and doing what's right for society is one of degrees.

Finally, some chief executives speak out publicly because of what might be called the spotlight effect. Narcissism, celebrity, and power can all factor into a leader's desire to communicate about social or political

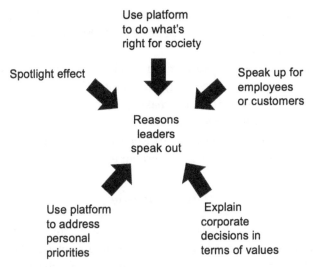

Fig. 1. Reasons Leaders Speak Out

issues.[41] For better or for worse, attention seeking is an undeniable part of the package, and social media has only contributed to this. MyPillow CEO Mike Lindell and Elon Musk are exhibits *A* and *B*, respectively, but this is hardly exclusive to right-leaning corporate leaders. Howard Schultz's ill-conceived "Race Together" initiative, which sought to have Starbucks employees engage with customers in conversations about race, was a case study of a charismatic leader selling his team a flawed idea.[42] Salesforce CEO Marc Benioff once quipped, "There is a third [political] party emerging in this country, which is the party of CEOs."[43] This love of the spotlight is not lost on the American public. One of the earliest polls on this topic found that a majority said CEOs take public positions on hotly contested issues either to get attention in the media (36 percent) or to build their personal reputations (21 percent).[44]

These five motivations offer an 80/20 model that can help explain why a CEO might speak out, but they don't address some circumstances. Some CEOs lead proactively on issues, while others only follow when there's a groundswell.[45] (See chapter 5 on fence-sitters.) And there are myriad examples of collective action, such as when nearly three hundred CEOs signed a letter in 2021 opposing a restrictive voting rights law in Georgia.[46] Joint efforts such as these offer reputational safety in numbers as well as the potential to have greater impact as part of a powerful group, but they also provide fewer opportunities to stand out from the crowd.[47]

With these varying motivations in mind, how should executives determine if, when, and how to say something? Above all, there should be a defined process for decision-making that considers what's at stake, who's affected by the issue, and what options are available. Chapter 10 offers a series of questions about *relevance, risks, values,* and *actions* that can serve as the basis for a framework for evaluating these choices.

How CEOs See It

CEOs around the world appear to be clear about one thing: social issues matter. A Bain & Company survey of three hundred global CEOs found that fully 85 percent say social issues are urgent for their businesses today, and six in ten cite "balancing the needs of all stakeholders" (39 percent) or creating "positive outcomes for society" (21 percent) as the primary role of their businesses.[48]

That doesn't mean all are equally comfortable speaking out. "For me to take, or for our company to take stances seems, quite frankly, silly because after all, companies are not meant to do that. Individuals do," said Microsoft CEO Satya Nadella.[49] In the same conversation, though, he noted that Microsoft "can definitely lend our voice, lend our support, push for legislation" on issues that affect it, including those that directly affect the health and welfare of its employees. "We will make sure we . . . protect our employees. That's our responsibility, and we'll be clear on that."

Until somewhat recently, many business leaders operated under a default assumption that talking publicly about anything political wasn't good for business. "This is unfamiliar terrain for CEOs," wrote Richard Edelman, noting that many business leaders are "more accustomed to working behind the scenes."[50]

The discomfort some CEOs feel about speaking out may be a function of their views of the private sector's role in society. GLG's 2023 survey of 458 CEOs around the globe found that income inequality (56 percent) was the one issue on which a majority of CEOs from all regions thought the private sector had the greatest responsibility to contribute to social progress.[51] Climate change also attracted support from a majority of leaders (52 percent), though CEOs in Europe, the Middle East, and Africa (61 percent) and the Asia-Pacific region (53 percent) felt much more strongly about this issue than leaders from the Americas (40 percent). Topics such as gender parity, racial justice, and immigration received less priority. It is worth noting that a majority of the CEOs surveyed by GLG lead companies with fewer than a thousand employees, but that shouldn't be seen as a reason to discount these results; there are far more leaders of small companies than of large ones.

Chief executives offer perfectly good reasons for steering clear of political or social issues in a divided country in which partisans increasingly distrust each other.[52] (See chapter 3.) An obvious concern is alienating customers, which Starbucks failed to appreciate with Race Together. As John Mackey of Whole Foods puts it, "One thing I've learned over the years is, we are so divided in politics, whatever I say is going to upset 50 percent of the population. So my own personal politics, I keep to myself."[53]

While this rationale is sound for any business trying to attract the broadest swath of the public, it's even more compelling for mission-based businesses offering a product or service that can be a matter of life or death for the customer. Jaime Vinck, CEO of Recovery Ways, which operates addiction treatment centers, noted that she consciously makes an effort not to express her own views on anything outside of mental health. "My job is to advocate for every single human being seeking treatment," she said. When mandatory COVID vaccination for employees emerged as an issue that required her to take a position, she saw that as within the scope of protecting patients rather than a matter of personal politics.[54]

Others characterize speaking out as a waste of time and energy. Brian Armstrong, cofounder and CEO of the crypto exchange Coinbase, attracted significant attention in September 2020 for stating that Coinbase, unlike many other Silicon Valley firms, would not take positions on broader societal issues. "The reason is that while I think these efforts are well intentioned, they have the potential to destroy a lot of value at most companies, both by being a distraction, and by creating internal division."[55]

Fred Voccola, CEO of the privately backed Kaseya, put it more bluntly in an introductory town hall with employees of Datto, which Kaseya had recently acquired. "Here's our company's strategy regarding social issues and political issues: We don't have an opinion. Period. We don't. We are not going to talk about Pride. We're not going to say Pride is bad. We're not going to talk about George Floyd, or say George Floyd is bad."[56]

Chief executives of companies with tens of thousands of employees, diversified operations, and a large global footprint face a more demanding landscape. "I think it's a corporate responsibility," said Doug Parker, former CEO of American Airlines.[57] "It's part of doing your job. And it really does have an impact on our business. If we're not making progress on important issues like infrastructure, if we're not making progress on important issues like race, that's not good for commerce. So you can justify it from a shareholder perspective if you need to. You can justify it on just doing what's right if you need to."

Some leaders see addressing political and social issues as an essential part of attracting and retaining high-quality employees in knowledge-based industries. "I think there is a huge responsibility for a CEO to be visible, for their voice to be heard, because talent is the most important thing to us," said Dana Maiman of IPG Health.[58] "It's so critical for people when they are joining an organization. They need to know what the organization stands for, and it all starts with the CEO and the vision that they're putting forth."

The question of what to address and when remains a challenging one. "It is the single biggest criticism I receive from my teammates: Why are you not commenting on everything that happened, because it's all outrageous and egregious and we're up in arms—Roe v. Wade, the war in Ukraine, senseless murders," said Evelyn Webster, CEO of SoulCycle.[59] "If I did what they asked me to do, I would comment on absolutely every world event."

A CEO's voice is a strategic asset. The key to using it effectively is picking spots selectively where it can have an impact. When CEOs are pressured to take a position on one issue or another, in most cases the answer should be a principled no.

The Sound of Silence

There are plenty of times when it is not advisable for a company to take a position on an issue. Any multinational that does business in countries with repressive political regimes will confront uncomfortable choices about sensitive subjects. "Some we do and some we don't. Some we can't," said Jamie Dimon, CEO of JPMorgan Chase, when asked how he makes decisions about which issues to address.[60]

Silence has its strategic uses. One example was evident in the different responses of Walgreens and CVS to warnings from twenty Republican state lawmakers about the sale of the abortion drug mifepristone in their states after the overturn of *Roe v. Wade*.[61] Walgreens told National Public Radio that it would not sell mifepristone in any of those states, including four in which the drug was still legal.[62] This prompted California governor Gavin Newsom to cancel a state contract with the pharmacy chain for what he characterized as its failure to stand up to "extremists."[63] (See chapter 4.) CVS said nothing at the time and steered clear of the political fallout.

*

But silence has its limitations. The approach of GM's Roger Smith in the late twentieth century was all about minimizing exposure. In a media landscape dominated by three broadcast networks, multiple daily newspapers, and a single cable news channel, information flowed at different volumes and velocities than it does today. Avoidance may have seemed like a good idea at the time, but Smith ended up drawing exactly the kind of attention he didn't want.

Technology has changed the calculus of silence. Journalists, consumers, employees, and issue advocates—all have multiple means at their fingertips to give them a voice with corporations and their executives. The line between internal and external communication has also blurred: every company-wide email or all-hands meeting can end up a news item. (Kaseya CEO Fred Voccola learned this when someone leaked a recording of his town hall meeting in which he protested, "I'm not being a dick," in response to a question. The headline wrote itself.[64])

One reason CEOs may feel compelled to speak out is because silence can be misinterpreted. "Will people maybe infer from your silence something that isn't your company's stance?" said Columbia University professor Vanessa Burbano.[65] "If every other company in your industry has come out and publicly made a statement on an issue, you don't want to be the one to stay silent." Delta Airlines CEO Ed

Bastian reached a similar conclusion after hesitating before speaking out against a restrictive Georgia voting law. "It's not possible to solely keep your head low, because if you keep your head low, that speaks also to people—not speaking," he said.[66]

In some cases, a proactive approach can counter the reputational risk of being on the wrong side of an issue or even the perception that this is the case. After Neil Young pulled his music from Spotify because the platform hosted episodes of Joe Rogan's podcast that spread misinformation about COVID vaccines, the company's stock price dropped 12 percent within a week.[67] Spotify CEO Daniel Ek's equivocation in a town hall meeting with employees—"We have to find the best possible way to balance creative expression with the safety of our listeners"—did nothing to change the narrative about Spotify or the short-term direction of its stock price.[68]

Another challenge with opting out is that the media keeps score. After Donald Trump's administration announced a travel ban against migrants from seven predominantly Muslim countries, more than a hundred tech CEOs signed an amicus brief protesting the ban.[69] Oracle, cofounded by Trump ally Larry Ellison, was notable in its absence from the brief. This led to a petition by Oracle employees that was subsequently covered by major outlets including *USA Today*, the *New York Times*, and the *Washington Post*.[70]

In some cases, silence can raise moral questions about leadership. On "important issues like race," said Doug Parker of American Airlines, "I can't imagine how you'd just stay on the sidelines and let it stay this way and not have a view, particularly when, like we had, people on our team reaching out and saying, no one's helping us here, can you help? Yeah, we'll help."[71]

*

There is an option between speaking and silence: communicating an explicitly apolitical position (e.g., "Vandelay Industries will not take a stance on this because we remain focused on our mission"). An experiment that examined responses to political events has found that depending on how stakeholders view a company's political leanings, an apolitical stance can go over better than silence in some instances and less so in others.[72] Values, expectations, and the division of opinion on the issue—all come into play when determining if an apolitical stance or silence is the better option.

Does Speaking Out Make a Difference?

It depends on who you ask. Employees and customers all have different expectations of chief executives, and they respond differently when leaders speak out. For each of these groups, the results are mixed. (At this point, the evidence is limited about its impact on suppliers, board members, politicians, regulators, and others.[73])

Where employees are concerned, CEOs benefit from high, steady levels of trust that employees have for their employers. The 2022 Edelman Trust Barometer found that 78 percent of employees across seven countries (including 78 percent in the United States) trust their employer. This has been relatively consistent over the past four years.[74]

This finding does not mean that employees blindly trust their leaders across the board. One set of issues on which CEOs in the United States face a significant credibility gap with younger employees is racism. While Edelman found in 2023 that a strong majority of employees (72 percent) trust their employer to do what is right when it comes to responding to systemic racism and racial injustice, there is a notable gap between the trust felt by executives (87 percent) and associates (67 percent).[75] And when it comes to straight talk about racism and DEI, employees at all career levels are most likely to believe someone who resembles the person they see in the mirror each morning. The CEO is *least trusted* to tell the truth about racism and DEI matters by associates (15 percent) and mid-level employees (24 percent), but they are most trusted by executives (56 percent). Conversely, associates (46 percent) and mid-level employees (56 percent) are most likely to trust "people like me."[76]

When it comes to job hunters, employees are attracted to companies that take stands that align with their views. Majorities of employees in the United States say they are more likely to work for a company if it publicly supports addressing a wide range of social issues, including human rights, racial justice, economic inequality, gender equality, and climate change. While Republicans and Democrats have clear differences, each of these issues has majority support from people of both parties. (Support falls off among Republicans on reproductive rights and gun safety.)[77]

As Dana Maiman of IPG Health concluded, a CEO's stance on issues matters to job seekers. When considering a job, three in five (60 percent) expect a CEO to speak out about issues they care about personally.[78] Support for this is actually higher among employees who are *less* secure in their employment (66 percent) than those who think they're unlikely to lose their jobs in the next year (59 percent), suggesting this expectation is not driven solely by pressure from employees who feel entitled to work in an ideological homogeneous environment.

Academic research offers more conflicting answers: speaking out can be a double-edged sword where employees are concerned.[79] As with customers, the key question is one of alignment with existing views. One study that analyzed evidence based on a real-world case found that a liberal stance from a CEO can either increase a liberal employee's commitment to a position they already hold, or it can harden a conservative's opposition.[80] An experiment that examined a closely related issue found a "demotivating effect" when employees disagreed with a CEO's stance and no significant gain among employees who supported the stance.[81] One question that neither of these studies can answer is if it matters how committed employees are to the issue in the first place. (For instance, would a CEO's position on the overturn of *Roe v. Wade* yield a different result than one on gender-neutral bathrooms?) While these and other studies don't yet provide definitive answers, common sense dictates that the risks of motivating some employees while alienating others are real. Evidence indicates that a sense of ideological alienation can lead to higher turnover rates.[82] The takeaway here is the importance of having a finger on the pulse of employee sentiment before taking a position.

With investors, the picture is also mixed. Some studies show that a CEO's position on an issue can drive gains in stock price.[83] Others find that a CEO's silence can lead investors to project their own views on that CEO.[84] While investors are clearly focused on earning returns, they have varying time horizons and agendas. Those that focus on start-ups, benefit corporations (B Corps), or social impact firms have priorities beyond the bottom line. Chapter 2 dives into the question of shareholders and stakeholders. An investor's perspective on that subject is probably a good proxy for her position on CEOs speaking out.

As far as customers go, multiple studies suggest that a CEO's stance can positively influence brand perceptions and intentions to purchase if customers share the CEO's point of view. Solid majorities of both Democrats (75 percent) and Republicans (59 percent) say they approve of companies that speak out on issues that are important to employees and customers.[85] The catch is that doing so can turn off customers who hold an opposing perspective.[86] A simple thought experiment about disagreement illuminates the risk: 40 percent of voters say they have boycotted a company because of its political or social stances, while only 35 percent have purchased from one in support of their stances.[87] "Cancel my subscription!" turns out to be somewhat stickier than "sign me up!" (See chapter 10 for more about customer math.)

As the public becomes increasingly accustomed to CEOs speaking out, caution is warranted for a couple reasons. First, there are generational differences around how much is too much. Half of boomers and 40 percent of Generation Xers (Gen Xers) think companies speak out too much these days, while far fewer millennials (31 percent) and Gen Zers (18 percent) agree.[88]

Second, the public is savvy to spin. A survey found that the vast majority of Americans (86 percent) say companies "often hide behind public declarations of support for stakeholders but don't walk the walk."[89] And a 2022 study of voters that involved follow-up interviews demonstrated a level of sophistication in calling out a say-do gap: "Some even pointed directly to Nike's vocal support of Black Lives Matter despite complacency in human rights violations for their workers in other countries."[90] The message couldn't be clearer: words matter, but they aren't enough.

2

SHAREHOLDERS AND STAKEHOLDERS

> The constant necessity to recognize public or national
> interest in all our business operations is a relatively new
> requirement for the businessman.
> —*Thomas J. Watson Jr., CEO, IBM, 1963*

Business leaders have always had to navigate the social and political context in which their firms operate. Sixty years ago, Coca-Cola president Robert Woodruff played a part in shifting the white Atlanta business community's narrative about civil rights. When the city's mayor sought to host a banquet in honor of Dr. Martin Luther King Jr., who had just won the Nobel Peace Prize, Woodruff came out in support of the mayor's effort.[1] Woodruff shouldn't be mistaken for a lifelong supporter of civil rights. The year after Rosa Parks was arrested for refusing to yield her seat on a bus, he backed the Senate candidacy of a white supremacist who deemed racial integration a Communist plot.[2] But a decade later, Woodruff's endorsement of King, along with other actions, played a part in helping Coca-Cola improve its standing with Black Americans. Woodruff's motivation was commercial: it was good for business.

Corporate engagement on political issues hasn't been limited to domestic affairs. Starting in the 1980s, over two hundred corporations divested from South Africa to put pressure on the apartheid regime.[3] Together with US sanctions, the reduction in American investment helped to force the South African government to realize that the ground beneath its feet had shifted.

And there's precedent for business leaders addressing political and social issues that are seemingly adjacent to their firm's core activities. During John F. Kennedy's administration, IBM CEO Thomas Watson Jr., wrote, "We can't simply say that inadequate medical care is the price people must pay if they are incapable of earning enough to provide for themselves."[4] Watson was a pragmatist about the role business leaders should play in accounting for concerns beyond earnings statements. "In planning for the future of our own particular interest, we must recognize the rights and requirements of the public and the millions of individuals who make it up."[5]

Relations between business and the public have tended to move in pendulum swings, as do efforts by corporate leaders to earn the public's trust. A half century before the tumult of the 1960s, in response to events including the fire at the Triangle Shirtwaist Company, a bombing at the *Los Angeles Times*' plant, and episodes of violence in the mining industry, business leaders met secretly in New York to address the nation's pervasive antibusiness sentiment.[6] The result was the establishment of the Conference Board, which tried to improve public support for business by sharing information. "Industry in this country must have the sympathetic support of the public," said Magnus W. Alexander, assistant to the president of General Electric (GE), in the *New York Times*.[7]

Watson versus Friedman

It's not likely that Woodruff or Watson would have used the term "stakeholder management" in the 1960s,[8] but each understood and practiced the concept. Woodruff's actions were a classic case of stakeholder engagement in service of shareholder value, while Watson espoused a brand of capitalism that accounted for the public good out of enlightened self-interest.

The question of whether business leaders should serve the interests of shareholders or stakeholders has been debated for decades. Watson rejected either-or thinking as a false choice: "We can render to our stockholders that which is theirs and at the same time do what we think is best for the country without bringing the two into head-on conflict."[9]

Watson's view reflected a perspective that had been articulated at the height of the Great Depression by Adolf Berle and Gardiner Means in *The Modern Corporation and Private Property*: "Neither the claims of ownership [shareholders] nor those of control [management] can stand against the paramount interests of the community."[10] Berle and Means offered this position as an alternative to either absolute fealty to shareholders or absolute control by managers. Thirty-five years later, in a new preface to *Modern Corporation*, Means nearly echoed Watson: "Profits are an essential part of the corporate system. But the use of corporate power solely to serve the stockholders is no longer likely to serve the public interest."[11]

Watson was not alone in believing that business had a role to play in serving the public interest. The societal changes of the 1960s challenged corporate America. Opposition to the Vietnam War on college campuses extended to protests against Dow Chemical, the manufacturer of napalm, and large manufacturing corporations wrestled with the perception of being pro-war.[12] The cultural shock waves from both the anti-war and liberation movements of the time led to a shift in tone. In General Electric's 1970 annual report, Chairman Fred Borch spoke of the "continuing effort to achieve an increasingly useful social role for General Electric," such as "helping solve urban and environmental problems," and "working intensively to enlarge our participation both in employing and training men and women from disadvantaged groups."[13] This was not a fringe effort: GE and IBM ranked number 4 and number 5, respectively, in the 1970 Fortune 500.[14]

Milton Friedman, America's most famous economist of the era, was having none of this. The author of the bestselling *Capitalism and Freedom* proclaimed in the title of a piece for the *New York Times Magazine* that "the social responsibility of business is to increase its profits."[15] In Friedman's view, the corporation's shareholders hired a chief executive "to conduct the business in accordance with their desires, which generally will be to make as much money as possible."

The crux of the theoretical argument behind this is what's commonly referred to as the "agency problem." Simply put, the job of a chief executive is to manage a company as the agent of its principals—the owners or stockholders. Any decision by a chief executive that doesn't maximize returns creates an "agency cost" for the owners.

From this perspective, a CEO taking a stance on a political or social issue that doesn't deliver value to shareholders is an agency cost. As always, there is a large gray area. For example, a CEO's position that attracts top talent to a firm or that motivates employee productivity can create shareholder value rather than diminishing it.[16]

The Friedman doctrine, as he called it, was a shot across the bow at anything that might be described as social responsibility, such as "eliminating discrimination, avoiding pollution," or other reforms that he dismissed as contemporary fads. From his vantage point, they constituted both a failure to act in pursuit of profit and a slippery slope toward socialism.

Some of the more nuanced points in Friedman's piece got lost in the noise. He acknowledged that it might serve the long-run interest of a corporation to put resources into "amenities" in communities in which it was a major employer, and he offered allowances for following the "ethical customs of society." In other words, management had the latitude to act on issues that would benefit a firm over time, as Robert Woodruff had done at Coca-Cola. But the headline about profits got all the attention.

Friedman's high-profile polemic was part of a growing conservative reaction to the sweeping changes of the 1960s. A year later, Lewis F. Powell Jr., soon to be nominated to the Supreme Court, wrote a confidential memo to a leader of the US Chamber of Commerce titled "Attack on American Free Enterprise System."[17] The Powell memo, as it became known, spelled out a broad, long-term counterattack agenda that included a comprehensive public relations strategy, and it approvingly quoted Friedman about the threat to freedom posed by "misguided individuals mindlessly parroting one another."

Friedman became synonymous with the gospel of shareholder supremacy, which, fortified by like-minded economists, won over a generation of managers and investors. A seminal paper by Michael C. Jensen and William H. Meckling acknowledged the inevitability of agency costs while stressing that "most organizations are simply legal fictions" consisting of a series of contracts: "Viewing the firm as the nexus of a set of contracting relationships among individuals also serves to make it clear that the personalization of the firm implied by asking questions such as 'what should be the objective function of the firm?' or 'does the firm have a social responsibility?' is seriously misleading. The firm is not an individual."[18]

This contract-centric approach reinforced Friedman's rejection of the social responsibility of business. It also implied that the way to minimize agency costs to owners was through arrangements that incentivized managers to make decisions as part owners rather than as employees.

As the focus on shareholders gained ascendancy in the 1980s, Jack Welch of General Electric became the CEO most closely identified with it. "What we have to sell to the equity investor is consistent, above-average earnings growth throughout the economic cycle," he wrote to his predecessor, Reginald Jones, when applying for the top role at GE.[19] (In the wake of the financial collapse of 2008, Welch did a public about-face on shareholder value, calling it "the dumbest idea in the world."[20]) Regardless of the extent of Welch's personal influence as an evangelist, the gospel spread. By 1985 a Booz Allen Hamilton survey found that half of CEOs (51 percent) cited creating shareholder value as their top priority.[21]

The Friedmanite worldview shaped the formative years of boomer and Generation X professionals who went to business school or entered the workforce in the last two decades of the twentieth century. "When I was younger, I would have said that the job of the CEO is to return value to shareholders. Period," said David Ehrlich, CEO of Aktana, an artificial intelligence–driven life sciences company.[22] "Nowadays, I tend to take a broader stakeholder view, understanding that workplaces are a pervasive form of social organization with societal impacts that extend beyond economics." Many of his contemporaries who came of age in the Ronald Reagan–George H. W. Bush era would agree.

Friedman's objection to the notion of corporate social responsibility points to the conflation of that concept with the dynamics that drive speaking out today. In 1981 Jeffrey Sonnenfeld distinguished between "social responsiveness," which he characterized as "a continuing state of awareness of public affairs and a readiness to comprehend them," and "social responsibility," or "the ethics of the corporation in a particular situation."[23] Friedman effectively lumped these ideas together

The shareholder primacy perspective was (and is) at its core profoundly American.

and dismissed both, reducing efforts such as GE's stated intention to diversify its workforce to a lack of focus on profits.

The shareholder primacy perspective was (and is) at its core profoundly American. European companies operate in a political and cultural context shaped by the European Social Charter, which addresses economic *and* social progress, human rights, and nondiscrimination in its preamble.[24] Similarly, the charter of Temasek Holdings, which has managed Singapore's sovereign wealth fund since 1974, emphasizes the importance of stewardship and delivering sustainable value over the long term.[25] In short, culture plays a large part in defining the questions that animate debates about the interests of shareholders and stakeholders.

Stakeholders, Stakeholder Capitalism, and Beyond

A couple years after Friedman put his stake in the ground, chief executives from General Electric, United States Steel, and other manufacturing and construction corporations formed the Business Roundtable, which stood up for some of the ideas that Friedman had rejected. It explicitly recognized that "the long-term viability of the business sector is linked to its responsibility to the society of which it is a part" and recommended that businesses determine how best to communicate their responsibilities to the public.[26]

The Business Roundtable also pursued priorities such as pushing back on government regulation and oversight,[27] but its founding generation of leaders, such as Reginald Jones of GE and Irving S. Shapiro of DuPont, understood the importance of harmonizing business interests with the public interest. "The Business Roundtable's thesis was that it was not antithetical to do good and do well," said Jeffrey Sonnenfeld of Yale University's Chief Executive Leadership Institute.[28] "Their whole spirit was to find an alignment of the goals of business and goals of society."

The Friedman view generated volleys of counterarguments in favor of a broader stakeholder perspective,[29] but a fully fleshed stakeholder-centric theory of management didn't emerge until a few years later. Professor R. Edward Freeman traced the first use of the term "stakeholder" to a 1963 internal memo at Stanford Research Institute.[30] He went on to develop a theory of strategic management that accounted for a wide range of stakeholders surrounding a CEO, including customers, suppliers, employees, governments, consumer advocates, environmentalists, and local communities, as well as the financial community.[31] "When things go badly," Freeman wryly noted, "the CEO stands squarely in the middle, shouldering the blame."

Freeman provided an intellectual framework that legitimized the importance of stakeholders in a strategic management context, and his unit of analysis was the firm. Other theorists looked at the question of which stakeholders matter most to CEOs and identified power, legitimacy, and urgency as the key attributes that CEOs consider when weighing stakeholder interests.[32]

Freeman didn't present his work as a theory of capitalism that could help address the world's most pressing problems. One of the best-known advocates for that idea was Klaus Schwab, founder and chairman of the World Economic Forum (better known as Davos).[33] Starting in the early 1970s, Schwab, like the Business Roundtable founders, pushed back against shareholder primacy, but he did so from a mountainside in Switzerland. While billionaires flying Gulfstreams halfway around the world to talk about reducing carbon emissions came to symbolize the Davos brand of stakeholder capitalism,[34] the term gained broader currency among business leaders as an approach that weighed stakeholder interests alongside those of shareholders. Related ideas such as purpose-driven capitalism and conscious capitalism offered different variations based on the theme.

From Public Interest to Self-Interest

As a CEO-led organization, the direction of the Business Roundtable evolved with the times. In the late 1990s, it issued a white paper that sounded like Friedman: "The principal objective of a business enterprise is to generate economic returns to its owners."[35] Among other things, changes in executive compensation now incentivized chief executives to focus on shareholder value more than in the past, and the Business Roundtable's stance reflected that shift.[36]

The Business Roundtable's pivot coincided with a broader failure of corporate leadership. As frauds perpetrated by Enron, WorldCom, and Tyco International prompted lawmakers to draft and pass the Sarbanes-Oxley Act of 2002, the business community focused on the burdens the new rules would impose rather than on taking a proactive role in shaping the legislation.[37] (Goldman Sachs CEO Hank Paulson was a notable exception.[38]) The Business Roundtable's statement to the House Committee on Financial Services on the pending legislation captured the tone of the era: it "supported the goal of stockholder protection" and trumpeted "the inherently self-correcting nature of our market system." The public interest was not part of the equation.[39]

Public confidence in big business fell at the time of these scandals, eventually hitting an all-time low by the end of the decade after the subprime mortgage crisis triggered the Great Recession.[40] As executives at financial firms that accepted government bailouts threatened to quit if their compensation was cut, and Goldman Sachs CEO Lloyd Blankfein said that bankers were doing "God's work,"[41] business leaders looked increasingly self-interested and out of touch with the pain the recession had caused on Main Street.

Winds of Change

As Wall Street's grumbling about bonuses gave way to Occupy Wall Street protests, broader changes were afoot. The advent of social media and smart phones radically democratized the flow of communication. Suddenly every human action or utterance could be captured in high-definition video. Citizens, consumers, and employees—all had a variety of outlets through which they could make their voices heard, with the virtual town square open to all on Twitter (now X), Facebook, LinkedIn, and other platforms.

A demographic shift was also underway. As boomers began to hit retirement age, the millennial generation started to make up a growing share of the workforce.[42] Over time, evidence supported what older leaders already knew: where political and social issues were concerned, millennials (and later Gen Zers) had different expectations of their bosses than did Gen Xers or boomers.[43]

The early 2010s saw social changes such as the movement for marriage equality for LGBTQ+ couples begin to gain broad public acceptance. While forward-thinking companies such as IBM and Disney began providing domestic partner benefits for all their employees in the mid-1990s,[44] the campaign for marriage equality fifteen years later called on a wide range of companies and CEOs to stand up for equal rights for their LGBTQ+ employees. Many answered the call. In 2012 forty-eight corporations signed an amicus brief saying that the Defense of Marriage Act (DOMA), which opposed gay marriage, was both discriminatory and bad for business: "DOMA imposes on amici not simply the considerable burden of compliance and cost. DOMA conscripts amici to become the face of its discrimination."[45] The following year over 275 corporations signed a brief in support of marriage equality.[46]

Around the same time, Google went beyond domestic politics with its "Legalize Love" campaign, which sought to promote the safety of its employees in countries with laws that threaten LGBTQ+ people: "Legalise Love is our call to decriminalise homosexuality and eliminate homophobia around the world."[47] This highlighted the challenge that multinational companies face protecting employees in countries that have legislated or institutionalized discrimination.

Starbucks's support for marriage equality led to a showdown at the 2013 annual meeting between then-CEO Howard Schultz and a shareholder who suggested that Schultz had wasted $10,000 supporting the issue instead of focusing on the stock price. Schultz shot back that the company had delivered a 38 percent shareholder return over the previous twelve months, saying that it was "not an economic decision" but rather one made "through the lens of our people." He finished with a challenge: "If you feel respectfully that you can get a higher return than the 38% you got last year, it's a free country. You could sell your shares at Starbucks and buy shares in other companies."[48] Starbucks's stock appreciated 315 percent over the next decade, significantly outperforming the S&P 500.[49]

Schultz wasn't the only CEO telling Friedmanites that they could park their dollars elsewhere. At Apple's 2014 annual meeting, a shareholder proposal from the conservative National Center for Public Policy

Research challenged CEO Tim Cook to commit only to business activities that would increase profits. Cook countered that Apple makes devices that are accessible to the blind, noting that he does so without considering the return on investment (ROI). "If you want me to do things only for ROI reasons, you should get out of this stock," he said.[50] As of this writing, Cook has created well over $2 trillion in shareholder value since that meeting.[51]

Four years later, when Levi Strauss CEO Chip Bergh prepared to take the company public, he told investors during the company's roadshow that it would engage on social and political issues just as it had in the past. Referring to a position Levi's had taken on ending gun violence in 2016, he recalled, "I looked investors in the eye and said, 'If you're uncomfortable with the company taking a stand on this, then we're not a company for you to invest in.'"[52]

The New Normal

Nearly a half century after Friedman's *New York Times* piece, the stakeholder view reached a high-water mark with the Business Roundtable's publication of its "Statement on the Purpose of a Corporation" in August 2019.[53] In a direct rejection of its 1997 position, the new statement positioned itself as a move "away from shareholder primacy." Instead, it endorsed "a fundamental commitment to all of our stakeholders." Singling out specific responsibilities to customers, employees, suppliers, and communities as well as shareholders, members committed to "deliver value to all of them." The statement specifically spoke of the need to "foster diversity and inclusion, dignity and respect" for employees and to "protect the environment by embracing sustainable practices," as well as "generating long-term value for shareholders."

While the business press hailed this as a major shift at the time,[54] others dismissed it as nothing more than talk. Two Harvard Law School professors conducted a survey of corporations that had signed the statement and noted that the CEOs did not seek board approval or ratification, concluding that the statement would not require corporations to make "any meaningful changes" in their treatment of stakeholders.[55] Two other early studies cast doubts about whether anything had changed. An analysis of firms that signed the statement revealed that in the first quarter of 2020, when COVID-19 was wreaking havoc across the globe, stock buybacks were on a par with early 2018 and early 2019.[56] Another found a mixed record: firms that signed the statement performed slightly worse than other firms in response to the COVID-19 crisis and slightly better than others in inequality performance.[57]

A longer time horizon may reveal a different story. Given the dramatic shifts in the Business Roundtable's positions over the decades, its 2019 statement is probably best understood as a barometer of CEO opinion. While refashioning the image of business was clearly a motivation, the CEOs who signed on also recognized definitively that the balance had shifted.

Nearly four years later, some traction with chief executives on a global level was evident. A Bain & Company survey of three hundred CEOs found a plurality (39 percent) saying that the primary role of their business was to "balance [the] needs of all stakeholders."[58] As Gardiner Means had predicted in 1967, the use of corporate power solely to serve shareholders would no longer serve the public interest.[59]

3

FILLING THE VOID

Why are business leaders now on the front lines of social and political issues that would have been off the radar a generation ago? The share-holder-stakeholder argument detailed in chapter 2 is a lagging indica-tor rather than an explanation in and of itself. Two broad trends have played a significant part in shaping this landscape: a decline in public trust in institutions and an increase in partisanship. As a result, CEOs have been pressed to act when political leaders have failed to protect their stakeholders or to make progress on key policy issues.

Trust

The United States has experienced a long-term decline in trust in insti-tutions that has spanned decades. Gallup has tracked public confidence in institutions for over forty years, and its aggregate measure of confi-dence in a range of major institutions fell by 44 percent between 1979 (48 percent) and 2022 (27 percent).[1] These institutions include orga-nized religion, the military, the Supreme Court, banks, public schools, newspapers, Congress, organized labor, and big business.

The institution not included in Gallup's average that has suffered the most precipitous decline in trust is the federal government. When IBM CEO Thomas Watson Jr. wrote in the early 1960s about the need for all Americans to have access to affordable medical care, he did so at a time when over 70 percent of Americans trusted the federal govern-ment to do the right thing.[2] Decades later, when Barack Obama worked to muster support for the Affordable Care Act, trust in the federal gov-ernment had fallen by roughly two-thirds.[3] Trust in government today is roughly comparable to what it was when the Affordable Care Act became law: as of May 2022, one-fifth of Americans (20 percent) expressed significant trust in the government.[4]

"Question authority," once a mantra of the Woodstock generation, is now the prevailing wisdom of American society as the baby boomers settle into retirement. The vast and varied reasons for this could fill a bookshelf. Robert Putnam wrote two decades ago about the fraying social fabric of American communities.[5] Scandals, from Watergate to the subprime mortgage crisis to the Catholic Church's coverup of pedophilia, all took a toll evident in trend surveys of trust by the Pew Research Center, Gallup, and others. The media landscape evolved from an analog past of three networks and local newspapers to a digital present in which individuals can choose news that suits their worldview. On top of that, deliberate efforts to spread disinformation on topics from abortion to climate change to presidential elections have stoked confusion and doubt among the public.[6]

This erosion of confidence in institutions such as organized religion or big business is not unique to the United States. As people lose trust in institutions that seem disconnected from their lives, they look for credible authorities and sources closer to home. For many, this search begins at the office. Over a four-year period from 2018 to 2022, Edelman found that employees in seven countries placed significantly more trust in their own employers than in business, nongovernmental organizations, government, the media, and other institutions.[7] And just as employers now are more trusted than the private sector in general, so are their executives. "As trust in institutions like the government and financial institutions has declined . . . people are looking to corporate leaders," said journalist-turned-media entrepreneur Katie Couric.[8]

But they turn not just to any corporate leader. In 2022 and 2023, Edelman surveyed residents of twenty-seven countries and found that roughly two out of three say they trust *their own* CEO, reflecting a significantly higher level of trust than in CEOs in general.[9] People expressed more trust in their own CEOs than anyone other than their coworkers and scientists. "There's been a shift in the way that people look to their leadership," said Michelle Rodriguez, director of diversity, inclusion, and belonging at LinkedIn.[10] "When you think about twenty or thirty years ago, people looked to their president, their civic leaders, as the primary leaders in their life. But now it almost feels like people are looking to their CEOs to fill that leadership presence in their lives."

With trust in business higher than trust in government, Edelman also found that global majorities are far more likely to say business is not doing enough on issues such as climate change and economic inequality than that business is overstepping its bounds.[11] Strong majorities expect CEOs to take public stands on climate change (82 percent), discrimination (80 percent), the wealth gap (77 percent), and immigration (72 percent).[12]

The lack of trust in institutions—particularly in government—has left CEOs filling a leadership void out of necessity rather than ambition. As Paul Polman, former CEO of Unilever put it, "Many have lost faith in politics to represent their views and secure their futures. They are turning to corporate power instead."[13] This helps explain why in 2022 Edelman found that two out of three people (68 percent) in fourteen countries (including 66 percent in the United States) say CEOs should take the lead on change rather than waiting for the government to impose change on them.[14]

Partisan Divide

During the same period that trust in institutions declined in the United States, political partisanship increased, dividing Americans into two camps that increasingly see each other as immoral, dishonest, and closed-minded.[15] Businesses struggle to manage these political dynamics. The Conference Board found that three-quarters of corporations described the political environment in the United States as extremely or very challenging, a two-thirds increase over two years (78 percent in 2023 versus 47 percent in 2021).[16] Whole Foods cofounder and CEO John Mackey noted the difficulty that this creates: "Government has to do its part. And that's a challenge right now because the country is so divided politically."[17]

The current level of partisanship did not grow in a vacuum; it was also stoked and exploited by political leaders. The Conference Board survey also found that corporations cite polarization and extremism among *policymakers* far more often than that among the *electorate* (89 percent versus 53 percent) as factors that make the political environment challenging for them.[18] Delta CEO Ed Bastian saw partisanship as a driver of the public's desire for private sector leadership. "The level of the divisiveness in our society has actually elevated corporate leaders to a higher position of credibility in the public's eye, particularly as political leaders have become unfortunately so partisan in their views," he said.[19]

Since Americans are deeply split on a host of political and social issues, it's not surprising that these differences extend to views on CEOs speaking out. As of 2021, eight in ten liberals (81 percent) said CEOs should take a stand on important issues, while roughly half as many (42 percent) conservatives agreed.[20] This mirrors a split about corporate stances on political issues. Between 2014 and 2018, there were strong partisan divisions about whether it was appropriate for corporations to take a stance on issues such as LGBTQ+ equality (80 percent Democrats versus 47 percent Republicans), transgender issues (76 percent Democrats versus 39 percent Republicans), and gun safety (83 percent Democrats versus 54 percent Republicans).[21] These findings stood in stark contrast with the near unanimity about taking a position on hiring and training military veterans (95 percent Democrats and 96 percent Republicans).

The partisan divide has colored Americans' perceptions of corporate brands. In 2022 Republicans cited Chick-fil-A and Hobby Lobby among the top five most reputable brands, while Democrats named Samsung and Target.[22] This is not altogether surprising; across twenty-seven countries, Edelman found that 63 percent buy or advocate for brands based on their beliefs and values.[23] While consumers may not follow through on this as consistently as survey results may suggest, the connection between political preferences and perceptions of brands makes sense to marketers. Companies such as Black Rifle Coffee, whose mission is "to serve coffee and culture to people who love America," or Jeremy's Razors, which promises customers that "every dollar you spend here is one less dollar in the pockets of woke CEOs,"[24] blend politics explicitly into their brand appeal. These kinds of marketing appeals aren't new—Ben & Jerry's excelled at them as an upstart independent company in the 1980s[25]—but at a time of high political polarization, it's not surprising that some brands are doubling down on partisan identity as a way of attracting customers.

Corporations cite polarization and extremism among policymakers far more often than that among the electorate as factors that make the political environment challenging for them.

While Hobby Lobby seems like a clear-cut case of alignment between a company's politics and its reputation among like-minded consumers, other brands such as Trader Joe's (number 1 overall in 2022) and Patagonia (number 3) have strong appeal on both sides of the aisle.[26]

Patagonia, which ascended from third place to first overall in the 2023 ranking,[27] is in its own category. The company has been unflinchingly liberal in its politics for decades. In 2022 founder Yvon Chouinard wrote, "Earth is now our only shareholder," as he announced that he and his family members had agreed to shift their ownership share of the company into a special-purpose trust to ensure that its profits would go to addressing climate change.[28] A year earlier, the company closed its store in Jackson Hole, Wyoming, after Jackson Hole Mountain Resort hosted a fundraiser for the House Freedom Caucus headlined by three Republican members of Congress who supported Donald Trump's false claims that he won the 2020 election.[29] Yet the brand is esteemed by both Republicans and Democrats alike. Patagonia may be simply an outlier whose broad appeal is driven primarily by positive feelings about its products. Whatever the reason, the company's overt politics have not interfered with the strength of its reputation among Americans of all political stripes.

The trend toward increased partisanship also shows up among business leaders: executives at the S&P 1500 have become more Republican in recent years. As of 2020, two-thirds of executives at these firms (68 percent) are Republicans (up five percentage points since 2008), and executive teams are more politically homogeneous than they were a dozen years ago.[30] This casts doubts on the hypothesis popularized by former Roivant CEO Vivek Ramaswamy that corporate America has been hijacked by a woke political agenda.[31] (See chapter 4, "The Empire Strikes Back.") Either many Republican executive teams are going along with ideas they find objectionable or the ideas aren't as objectionable as Ramaswamy and like-minded allies insist they are in the first place.

These executive teams may find these ideas acceptable because they see the business value in speaking out in certain situations. An analysis found that a significant number of CEOs who are Republican donors in their personal lives speak out in their professional roles in favor of social causes that are typically considered liberal.[32] This contradicts the notion that CEOs' political beliefs drive their corporate positions. It is also consistent with findings from Yale's Chief Executive Leadership Institute that deemphasize the importance of partisan identity. "Our recent research at the Yale School of Management into companies' responses to the overturning of *Roe v. Wade* showed rather that these were rarely driven by the personal politics of a given boss. Instead, industry, geography, the workforce and a firm's customer base largely determined company positions," wrote Jeffrey Sonnenfeld.[33] In a nation in which pluralism and partisanship coexist in an uneasy tension, basing these decisions on one individual's political leanings is a recipe for unhappiness.

When Political Leaders Fail to Protect Stakeholders

The issues that galvanized CEOs to speak out in the mid-2010s often emerged in response to conservative legislation at the state level. In 2015 after Indiana passed the Religious Freedom Restoration Act, which opened the door for businesses to discriminate against LGBTQ+ people, Salesforce CEO Marc Benioff announced that the company would reduce its investment in the state.[34] Within a week, other corporate leaders with a strong presence in the state including Roche Diagnostics, Dow AgroSciences, and Cummins registered their opposition in a letter to then-governor Mike Pence.[35] Dozens of Benioff's peers, including CEOs from tech companies ranging from Microsoft to Netflix, signed a public letter.[36] Benioff went on to support relocating employees, sending a $50,000 check to one who asked for assistance to move because that person didn't "feel comfortable living in this state anymore."[37]

Similarly, in 2016 over 130 CEOs signed a letter opposing North Carolina's House bill 2, which prevented transgender people from using the public restroom consistent with their gender identity. Companies endorsing the letter ranged from Northrop Grumman to Pfizer.[38] PayPal canceled a planned expansion in Charlotte that would have added four hundred jobs.[39] The law "violates the values and principles that are at the core of PayPal's mission and culture," said CEO Dan Schulman.[40] The CEOs' position was not without political risk: polling showed that North Carolinians held more conflicted views about the bill at the time.[41]

The election of Donald Trump presented a more complicated landscape for corporations that disagreed with specific policies but wanted to maintain ties with the administration. Intel, for instance, was one of more than a hundred companies that signed an amicus brief opposing Trump's February 2017 travel ban against migrants from seven predominantly Muslim countries, even though CEO Brian Krzanich was also a member of the president's American Manufacturing Council at that time.[42]

The tension between corporate leaders and the White House reached a breaking point that August 2017 after Trump remarked that there was "blame on both sides" for a white supremacist rally in Charlottesville, Virginia, that resulted in the death of a counterprotester.[43] Merck CEO Kenneth Frazier was the first to announce he was leaving the American Manufacturing Council. In a tweet, Frazier said, "As CEO of Merck and as a matter of personal conscience, I feel a responsibility to take a stand against intolerance and extremism."[44] Krzanich and others soon followed,[45] and the council collapsed as a result.

The political leadership vacuum reached its nadir in the immediate aftermath of the 2020 election, starting with Donald Trump's false claims of election fraud. Many CEOs strongly condemned the January 6 insurrection, and dozens of corporations and trade associations announced a pause in political action committee (PAC) contributions to lawmakers who continued to contest the election results.[46]

But the situation that pushed hundreds of CEOs to take a stand was a Georgia law passed in March 2021 that restricted voter access through measures such as making it harder for voters to obtain absentee ballots and limiting the number and location of absentee ballot drop boxes.[47] While executives such as Marc Benioff of Salesforce and Brad Smith of Microsoft voiced their clear and early opposition to the bill, CEOs of corporations headquartered in the state such as Coca-Cola and Delta remained silent.[48]

Kenneth Frazier, recently retired as CEO of Merck, and Kenneth Chenault, retired CEO of American Express, felt compelled to step into the void. They had each earned the greatest levels of respect from their peers and were free of the pressures of sitting CEOs who had to answer to boards and investors. Together they led seventy-two Black executives to publish a letter titled "Memo to Corporate America: The Fierce Urgency Is Now."[49] (See chapter 7, "Lived Experience Matters," for more on this issue.)

Chenault pointed out in the *New York Times* that while dozens of companies had signed a statement the previous year opposing legislation harmful to LGBTQ+ people, issues affecting Black Americans faced a double standard. "It is bizarre that we don't have companies standing up to this," he said.[50]

The same day the letter appeared, the CEOs of Coca-Cola and Delta, facing threats of boycotts, each reversed course and voiced opposition to the law.[51] Delta's position immediately resulted in political retaliation: the Georgia General Assembly voted to strip the airline of a tax exemption on jet fuel valued at $35 million.[52]

The dam appeared to break. Major League Baseball announced it was moving the All-Star Game, which was slated to take place in Atlanta.[53] The campaign that Black executives started to enlist the business community's support culminated with a statement signed by seven hundred firms that ran as a paid, two-page spread in the *New York Times, Washington Post, Wall Street Journal,* and *USA Today.*[54]

The Georgia law wasn't the only statewide effort to limit voting access that sparked a corporate response. Texas legislators also pushed forward a bill that, among other things, prohibited state employees from using funds to encourage voters to request mail-in ballots.[55] It prompted opposition from more than fifty companies, including American Airlines, Microsoft, HP, Levi Strauss, and Unilever.[56]

The events of those early months of 2021 should be put into context. In January, for the first time in American history, a defeated president took active steps to resist the will of the voters and the peaceful transfer of power, culminating in an armed insurrection to disrupt that process. The laws in Georgia and Texas that restricted or complicated voting subverted the most fundamental right of citizens in a democratic republic. These extraordinary events then placed extraordinary demands on leaders. If this analysis seems overblown, recall that the 2022 midterm elections took place largely without incident or the collective involvement of hundreds of CEOs.

While many corporate leaders took principled stands during that period, there was clear-eyed calculus in some of their positions as well. For instance, corporations operating in highly polarized states were more likely than other firms to pause PAC donations to election-denying members of the House and Senate after the January 6 insurrection.[57] The pause in PAC donations in early 2021 was also just that: only a fraction of the corporations that pledged to stop donations to those members of Congress who voted against certifying the election kept their pledges.[58]

Abortion posed different dynamics than voting rights. With the Supreme Court's decision to overturn *Roe v. Wade* in June 2022, business leaders faced the challenge of protecting employees' access to abortion care while knowing that support for the issue could jeopardize alienating a nontrivial minority of the public.[59] The reversal of *Roe* made abortion illegal immediately in several states, creating a complicated picture for companies with employees located throughout the country.

Texas had already put companies on notice in 2021 by passing one of the nation's most restrictive abortion laws in the country.[60] Corporations with offices in the state had to determine if and how to make abortion care available to their employees. In response, over fifty companies signed a statement opposing the restrictions,[61] but few went public about covering employees' costs to travel to other states for care.

Microsoft was one of the exceptions. "We were very, very clear at Microsoft that we will support women's choice—their rights—on any medical decisions they make. Therefore, our insurance will cover them wherever they want to go and exercise that right," said CEO Satya Nadella.[62]

Other tech companies proposed different solutions. Bumble and Match, both headquartered in Texas, each set up relief funds to support state residents seeking abortions.[63] Salesforce CEO Marc Benioff offered to help employees relocate out of Texas. "Ohana if you want to move we'll help you exit TX. Your choice," he tweeted, using the Hawaiian word "ohana," which translates broadly as "family."[64]

As soon as a draft of the court's majority opinion overturning *Roe* leaked in early May 2022, some executives and companies spoke loudly and clearly. Facebook chief operating officer Sheryl Sandberg called it "a scary day for women all across our country."[65] The following day, Levi Strauss let employees know that they were already eligible for reimbursement if they had to travel to access health care not available in their home states, including abortion. It framed the announcement as "a business imperative," noting that women compose 58 percent of its global workforce.[66] Bank of America CEO Brian Moynihan's support was more indirect. He characterized *Roe* as "the settled law of the land" before saying, "We believe people should have that access."[67]

But most business leaders remained silent. A couple weeks after the leaked opinion, Fast Company polled two hundred companies on the subject and received only fifteen responses.[68] Even after the court released its decision, many CEOs did their best to steer clear of the subject. Douglas McMillon, CEO of Walmart, the nation's largest employer, wrote internally that the company was "working thoughtfully and diligently to figure out the best path forward."[69]

Over a hundred companies said they would cover costs for employees to travel out of state for abortions.[70] The details of who could and couldn't access these benefits revealed a broader story of socioeconomic inequity: in many cases, the coverage did not extend to lower-paid workers or contractors.[71] Hundreds more companies signed a statement affirming support for abortion care,[72] but relatively few CEOs addressed the topic head-on. A Conference Board survey of three hundred companies in the weeks immediately after the decision found that just 10 percent had made or planned to make a public statement.[73] Where abortion was concerned, executives decided it was best to serve their employees and say nothing.

Two companies squarely in the line of fire on this issue were CVS and Walgreens. In early 2023, after the US Food and Drug Administration made it possible for retail pharmacies to dispense mifepristone—one of two drugs commonly used in combination to terminate early pregnancies—twenty Republican attorneys general signed joint letters to each company warning them to adhere to the letter of federal law regarding the dispensing of the drug.[74] (The attorney general of Kansas sent a separate letter.[75])

In response, Walgreens said it would not sell mifepristone in any of those states, despite the fact that abortion remained legal in four of them.[76] Then-CEO Rosalind Brewer did not comment publicly. In an internal memo, she acknowledged that people had "deeply-held beliefs" on the issue and said that Walgreens planned to dispense the drug where it was legal and not where it was illegal.[77] (See chapter 4 for California governor Gavin Newsom's response to Walgreens.)

A few weeks later, CVS CEO Karen Lynch took a different approach when asked by journalist Hope King how CVS planned to respond to the letter. "We have been a strong proponent for many years in women's health. What we have said is that we will dispense drugs that are FDA-approved where legally permissible," Lynch said. "Just look at the numbers with maternal health in America. It is unacceptable that a country of ours is going backwards in maternal health. We need to make sure that people and women are getting the care and the services that they need. End stop."[78] The substance of her response was fundamentally the same as Brewer's—the company would dispense the drug where legal—but her framing spoke to values. (See chapter 8, "Values Matter.")

Regardless of the differences in the two CEOs' responses, the issue demonstrated that corporations were still being drawn into the fray as a consequence of conservative politicians' actions at the state level.

When Policy Falls Short

As the scientific consensus hardened around the problem of carbon pollution,[79] climate change exposed a failure of US political leaders to enact policies commensurate with the size and scope of the problem. The Obama administration found itself limited to actions that didn't require Congressional approval, and Donald Trump ran for office promising to undo any progress Obama had made.[80] A manager or an investor who concluded from the science that climate change represented a strategic risk to long-term value could not reasonably expect the federal government to help mitigate it.

"I really think that climate change is the biggest threat that we all face. And I believe that we cannot expect governments and people around us to solve the problem. And I think it's time all corporate leaders and companies embrace that mind-set, and many are," said Niren Chaudhary, CEO of Panera,[81] echoing some of the notes of Larry Fink's 2020 letter to CEOs.

While Patagonia may have set the gold standard for taking matters into its own hands, investor-owned firms face greater pressures to balance climate objectives with the profit motive. As a result, many corporations and investors are tackling sustainability both at the firm level and through networks such as Ceres and globally through initiatives such as the Glasgow Financial Alliance for Net Zero and the United Nations–backed Race to Zero campaign. (See chapter 9 for more about these endeavors and their political detractors.)

The limitation of this approach, of course, is its reliance on voluntary action. Institutional investors have leverage over portfolio companies as well as a fiduciary responsibility to their customers. And with almost two-thirds of global Fortune 500 companies announcing 2050 emissions targets and with nearly half setting 2030 goals,[82] concerns about "greenwashing"—that is, saying one thing and doing another—are real.

At the same time, heightened expectations around sustainability reporting have raised the stakes and should act as a check on widespread false claims. "In today's very transparent world, it's really hard to get away with anything for very long," wrote Mark Tercek, CEO of the Nature Conservancy from 2008 through 2019.[83]

For now, the voluntary approach places a lot of weight on enlightened leadership. "We touch a lot of companies around the world because we manufacture things, and we know that we have a responsibility to convince those companies to use renewable energy, and to recycle, and to do things that are sustainable," said Apple's Tim Cook.[84] Apple has long been ahead of the corporate pack on climate change: it left the US Chamber of Commerce in 2009 over the chamber's opposition to proposed federal action to regulate carbon through the Clean

Air Act.[85] Reliance on the courage of individual leaders will only move the needle so far.

With over $100 trillion in global assets under management now committed to net-zero goals,[86] the only path toward bridging the current policy gap is for investors and CEOs to speak in favor of smart regulation, to work through trade associations to do the same, and to align their political contributions accordingly. In Mark Tercek's words, "The best way for investors to achieve net-zero portfolios is for them to lobby hard for tough regulatory climate policy."[87]

The difficulty of pushing back on policy failures resulting from political gridlock is the inevitable battle with the entrenched interests protecting the status quo. Gun violence is another issue that prompted corporate responses to federal government inaction. The problem is more than a series of headlines. As of this writing, the United States accounts for nearly three-quarters (73 percent) of mass shootings in developed countries, and it ranks first in firearms homicides among high-income countries with populations of 10 million or more.[88] As noted in chapter 1, Howard Schultz of Starbucks wrote a letter in 2013 titled "Our Respectful Request" that politely asked customers not to bring weapons into the company's stores.[89] More recently, CEOs in a wide range of industries have spoken out on this issue.[90] As Apple experienced with the Chamber of Commerce on climate change, resistance has come from the parties with the most to lose. Fossil fuels and firearms are the twin industries that ignited a backlash that has since extended far and wide.

4

THE EMPIRE STRIKES BACK

Larry Fink's 2020 letter to CEOs did not go unanswered. A year later, Texas legislators introduced Senate bill (SB) 13, which called for a "prohibition on investment in financial companies that boycott certain energy companies."[1] Its expansive definition of a boycott included "taking any action that is intended to . . . limit commercial relations with a company" in the fossil fuel industry. The bill called for state retirement or pension funds to divest from financial firms that the state comptroller deemed out of compliance. The message to BlackRock and others was clear: the war against environmental, social, and governance (ESG) principles, including any action to address climate change, was on.

Other states with significant economic interests in fossil fuels, including West Virginia, Kentucky, and Oklahoma,[2] passed similar laws. When West Virginia treasurer Riley Moore announced that BlackRock, Goldman Sachs, JPMorgan Chase, Morgan Stanley, and Wells Fargo would be ineligible for state banking contracts, he wrote, "Any institution with policies aimed at weakening our energy industries, tax base and job market has a clear conflict of interest in handling taxpayer dollars."[3] It didn't matter that an annual report coauthored by a consortium of environmental organizations including the Sierra Club ranked JPMorgan (number 1), Wells Fargo (3), Morgan Stanley (12), and Goldman Sachs (14) among the biggest bankers to fossil fuel companies from 2016 to 2021.[4] The talking point was that net-zero goals posed an existential threat to the industry.

Such attacks began to have a chilling effect on corporate communication about sustainability. A 2022 survey of twelve hundred global companies found that nearly one quarter (23 percent) were "greenhushing"; that is, they maintained net-zero goals but chose not to publicize them.[5]

The legacy energy sector wasn't the only one looking to politicians to retaliate against CEOs and companies that took action on any issues under the ESG umbrella. Gun manufacturers also sought protection. Texas's companion to SB 13 was SB 19, which "prohibited contracts with companies that discriminate against the firearm or ammunition industries."[6] SB 19 penalized banks that placed any restrictions on firearms companies by shutting them out of Texas's massive municipal bond market. Both laws went into effect in September 2021.

JPMorgan Chase and Citi, two of the banks that would be ineligible under the new law to underwrite municipal bonds in Texas, claimed they did not discriminate against firearms companies. At the same time, neither bank announced a change in its business practices with gunmakers. "We have been consistent in our position that we do not finance manufacturers of military-style weapons for civilian use," said a spokesperson for JPMorgan Chase.[7]

As with all wars, the backlash laws came at a very real cost. Economists at the Wharton School and the Federal Reserve Bank of Chicago estimated that by limiting competition among banks, Texas taxpayers ultimately faced $300 million to $500 million in higher borrowing costs.[8] A follow-up study of Kentucky, Florida, Louisiana, Oklahoma, West Virginia, and Missouri found increased costs ranging from tens of millions to hundreds of millions per state.[9] The banks excluded from bidding in these states could legitimately argue that these laws, and others like them, were anti-free market.

The banking industry also took countermeasures against these attacks. After Kentucky's state attorney general announced an antitrust investigation into six of the biggest banks for their involvement in the United Nations' Net-Zero Banking Alliance, the bankers fired back, filing a suit claiming that the attorney general had created "an ongoing state surveillance system" and violated the banks' constitutional rights to free speech and free association.[10]

The Backlash Playbook

Just as there's nothing new about corporate involvement in the issues of the day, neither are the political backlashes for their decisions. In an incident that now seems like past as prologue, fifteen Florida legislators wrote a letter to Disney chairman Michael Eisner in 1995 protesting the company's decision to offer domestic partner benefits to same-sex partners of employees: "We strongly disapprove of your inclusion and endorsement of a lifestyle that is unhealthy, unnatural and unworthy of special treatment."[11] Two years earlier, Apple faced opposition from the commissioners of Williamson County, Texas, for implementing the same policy for its employees. The commissioners voted first to rescind a tax break for Apple but reversed course a week later after Apple agreed to go ahead with plans to build a new customer support center in the county that would create seven hundred jobs.[12]

The playbook for the current backlash was road tested in the state of Georgia in 2018. After a mass shooting at Marjory Stoneman Douglas High School in Parkland, Florida, killed seventeen people, Georgia-based Delta Airlines announced that it would cancel a passenger discount for travel to the annual meeting of the National Rifle Association (NRA).[13] The Georgia state legislature retaliated by voting to strip Delta of a tax break on jet fuel worth $50 million.[14] Delta disclosed that only thirteen passengers had ever taken advantage of the discount,[15] but the numbers made no difference. The playbook was clear: Republican politicians would use the power of the state to penalize any corporate action on a social issue deemed a threat to their interests. In this case, Georgia's interests were identical to those of the NRA.

Delta was far from the only corporation to take a stance after the Parkland shooting. Dick's Sporting Goods announced that it would no longer sell assault rifles or high-capacity magazines in its stores, and it raised its buying age to twenty-one. "We're going to take a stand and step up and tell people our view and, hopefully, bring people along into the conversation," said then-CEO Ed Stack.[16]

Citi was the first bank to act. It mandated that its business customers raise the buying age to twenty-one, conduct background checks, and discontinue the sale of bump stocks and high-capacity magazines.[17] "Banks serve a societal purpose—we believe our investors want us to do this and be responsible corporate citizens," said CEO Michael Corbat.[18] Other banks, including JPMorgan Chase and Bank of America, followed suit with their own policy changes.[19] Three years later, all three found themselves in the crosshairs of SB 19.

The War on ESG and the War on Woke

In addition to anti-boycott laws specifically protecting fossil fuel and firearms companies, a broader class of legislation and executive actions targeting ESG began to appear. By one count, thirty-seven states introduced 165 distinct anti-ESG bills in the first half of 2023 alone.[20] As of mid-2023, twenty-three states had passed some type of anti-ESG legislation, and several others had adopted position statements.[21] (See "The Other Side of the Coin" section in this chapter regarding pro-ESG legislation.)

Action occurred at the federal level as well. In May 2022, Rep. Chip Roy (R-TX) introduced the "No ESG at TSP" Act, which would have prohibited ESG investments under the Thrift Savings Plan, a retirement savings plan similar to a 401k account for federal employees and uniformed military service members.[22] While Roy's bill gained no traction when Democrats controlled the House of Representatives, anti-ESG sentiment was welcome under new House leadership after the midterm elections: in March 2023, the Republican majority voted to nullify a Department of Labor rule that permits fiduciaries to consider ESG factors in private sector employee retirement plans.[23]

Florida governor Ron DeSantis made clear that his opposition to ESG was about more than defending his state's economic interests. In directing fund managers of Florida state pensions not to include ESG considerations in their investment decisions, he said, "Corporate power has increasingly been utilized to impose an ideological agenda on the American people through the perversion of financial investment priorities under the euphemistic banners of environmental, social, and corporate governance and diversity, inclusion, and equity."[24] A few months later, Florida's chief financial officer (CFO) announced that the state was divesting $2 billion from BlackRock.[25]

DeSantis's action on state pensions came a day after a federal judge had blocked his "Stop WOKE" Act, which sought to "take on both corporate wokeness and Critical Race Theory in schools in one act."[26] In his injunction, US District Court judge Mark E. Walker compared the state of First Amendment law in Florida to the topsy-turvy world of the Netflix series *Stranger Things*: "Normally, the First Amendment bars the state from burdening speech, while private actors may burden speech freely. But in Florida, the First Amendment apparently bars private actors from burdening speech, while the state may burden speech freely."[27]

DeSantis lost that battle, but it was just one in a larger, multifront war against corporate efforts to promote diversity, equity, and inclusion. Earlier that year, he signed the Parental Rights in Education Act,[28] which became widely known as the "Don't Say Gay" bill because of its prohibitions on discussing sexuality in schools. This drew him into direct conflict with Disney, which has tens of thousands of employees in the state and generates billions in economic activity.

There was an important distinction between DeSantis's retribution against Disney and other states' actions to defend the fossil fuel and firearms industries: West Virginia was pushing back on changes in business practices that affected its economic interests; DeSantis was sanctioning a dissenting voice. (See chapter 5, "Doers, Talkers, Fence-sitters, and Straddlers," for a detailed discussion of this case.)

If DeSantis was the politician most eager to brand himself a culture warrior, his private sector peer was Vivek Ramaswamy, the former CEO of Roivant Sciences who rose to fame as the author of *Woke, Inc.: Inside Corporate America's Social Justice Scam*. He used the word "diversity" 215 times in the book, writing about his difficulties connecting with Roivant's employees after the murder of George Floyd while at the same time asserting, "I don't believe in systemic racism."[29] In early 2023, Ramaswamy joined DeSantis in the race for the Republican presidential nomination in 2024,[30] clearly indicating the former's appetite for the spotlight.

It is no accident that DeSantis, Ramaswamy, and like-minded allies branded their opposition to everything from gay rights to reducing greenhouse gasses as "anti-woke." They chose a word that came up through Black culture as a positive quality, gained increasing popularity in the 2010s, and became ubiquitous after the Black Lives Matter protests following George Floyd's murder in May 2020.[31] It was unmistakably a word of the political left, and to those unclear about its meaning, it sounded amorphous enough to be weaponized in the culture wars. Recognizing that support for Black Lives Matter is po-

> There was an important distinction between DeSantis's
> retribution against Disney and other states' actions to
> defend the fossil fuel and firearms industries:
> West Virginia was pushing back on changes in business
> practices that affected its economic interests;
> DeSantis was sanctioning a dissenting voice.

larized—roughly half of white Americans have expressed opposition to Black Lives Matter since September 2020[32]—the culture warriors crafted a twenty-first-century dog whistle intended to cast anything they deemed "woke" in an unfavorable light with a significant slice of the American public.

Evidence indicated that these efforts to brand speaking out on political and social issues as "wokeness" was working. A poll taken after the 2022 midterm elections found that a narrow majority (52 percent) of American voters agreed with the statement that "corporate wokeness has gone too far."[33] The gray area was voters' definition of what constitutes "corporate wokeness," but clearly some of the criticism by leaders such as DeSantis was having its intended effect. At the same time, the study found that "neither Republican nor Democratic voters support policymakers' potential legislative efforts to curb ESG initiatives."[34]

DeSantis wasn't the only politician stoking these flames. In 2023 JPMorgan Chase faced heat from fourteen Republican state treasurers for "an apparent pattern of political bias" that could "impair the freedom of its customers to access financial services without fear of discrimination."[35] Nineteen Republican attorneys general followed by charging that the bank had "persistently discriminated against certain customers due to their religious or political affiliation" despite its stated commitment to inclusivity.[36] The company categorically denied all accusations of religious discrimination but provided no details about the specifics.

The culture war against corporations spread beyond the political class. In the spring of 2023, right-wing social media activists organized boycotts of Bud Light, Target, and North Face in attempts to intimidate the companies into abandoning their efforts to reach LGBTQ+ customers, particularly around Pride month.[37] (See chapter 5 for more about the responses of Bud Light and Target.) Even Chick-fil-A, owned and led by evangelical Christian Dan Cathy and rated the topmost reputable brand by Republicans a year earlier, came under fire from conservatives on social media simply for having a DEI program for its employees.[38]

With the boycotted companies on the defensive, like-minded politicians piled on. Seven Republican attorneys general said that Target Corporation was "the subject of a campaign by left-wing activist 'stakeholders' supporting an 'LGBTQIA+' agenda" and insinuated that its financial losses resulting from the boycott demonstrated a failure of its fiduciary duty to act in the best interests of shareholders.[39] DeSantis leveled a similar charge at the parent company of Bud Light.[40]

The boycotts and ensuing political attacks did not go unanswered. More than seventy-five companies, including Dow, Xerox, Pfizer, and Molson Coors, signed a statement condemning anti-LGBTQ+ legislation and affirming their commitment to their LGBTQ+ employees, clients, and customers.[41] Target got a boost from fifteen Democratic attorneys general who expressed support for the company and urged it "to double down on inclusivity, reject hate in all its forms, and stand firm in the face of intimidation and discrimination."[42]

The next front in the culture war against corporations opened after the Supreme Court's dismantling of affirmative action in university admissions.[43] Many of the same politicians who had taken on JPMorgan Chase and Target felt emboldened by the court's legal reasoning to challenge corporate efforts to promote diversity, equity, and inclusion. Two weeks after the court handed down its decision, thirteen Republican attorneys general wrote an open letter to the CEOs of Fortune 100 companies warning them "to refrain from discriminating on the basis of race, whether under the label of 'diversity, equity, and inclusion' or otherwise."[44] The letter explicitly cited Microsoft, JPMorgan Chase, and others that had made pledges to increase diversity after the murder of George Floyd.

Along the same line, Sen. Tom Cotton (R-AR) cited the court's decision in a warning to Target Corporation CEO Brian Cornell that a failure to end the company's "race-based employment and partnership practices" would likely result in litigation.[45] Cotton's letter, like the one by the Republican attorneys general, glossed over the fact that Chief

Justice John Roberts's majority opinion in the case cited Title VI (education) of the 1964 Civil Rights Act rather than Title VII (employment). But that was beside the point: both letters signaled loudly and clearly that corporate DEI initiatives were under fire.

The War on BlackRock and Larry Fink

Ramaswamy's enthusiasm for serving as a self-described "traitor to his class" led billionaires Peter Thiel and Bill Ackman to stake him as the CEO of Strive, an asset management fund that sought to position itself staunchly in the Friedmanite tradition.[46] "We will tell oil companies to be excellent oil companies and coal companies to be excellent coal companies and solar companies to be excellent solar companies," Ramaswamy said.[47] The code name for Strive before its public unveiling was "Whitestone," signaling its founders' antipathy toward the world's largest asset management firm. (Ramaswamy stepped down as the head of Strive in 2023 to run for president.)

Ramaswamy was not the only one taking aim at BlackRock. Consumer's Research, a conservative advocacy organization, initiated a multimillion-dollar campaign to discredit the firm.[48] Nineteen Republican attorneys general, led by Arizona attorney general Mark Brnovich, signed a letter protesting BlackRock's "quixotic climate agenda" and alleging antitrust concerns because of the firm's participation in the Climate Action 100+ and Glasgow Financial Alliance for Net Zero networks.[49]

The war became increasingly personal. A few months after Texas's SB 13 became law, Texas lieutenant governor Dan Patrick wrote a letter to state comptroller Glenn Hegar about the firms he should target: "As you prepare the official list of companies that boycott energy companies, I ask that you include BlackRock, and any company like them."[50] He used zero-sum logic: "Just yesterday, BlackRock Chairman and CEO, Larry Fink, issued his annual 2022 letter to CEOs indicating that BlackRock's goal is to transition to a 'net zero' world, including decarbonizing the energy sector. Needless to say, it is highly inconsistent to claim support for Texas' oil and gas energy industry while leading a 'net zero' policy effort that will destroy the oil and gas industry and destabilize the economy worldwide."

North Carolina treasurer Dale Folwell called for Fink's removal as the head of BlackRock. Arguing that Fink was driving the firm to violate its duty, Folwell wrote: "At Larry Fink's direction, BlackRock has used the financial power of its clients to force the global warming agenda, using proxy voting authority to push companies to 'net zero,' often in conflict with its fiduciary responsibilities."[51]

While Folwell accused BlackRock of failing in its role as a fiduciary, other states bumped against a different reality based in dollars and cents. A fiscal impact statement prepared for the Indiana state legislature found that divesting from investment managers who pursue ESG strategies could cost the state's retirement funds $6.7 billion over a decade.[52] The House of Representatives of North Dakota, which ranks second in the nation in crude oil reserves after Texas, voted 90–3 against a bill to create a boycott list similar to the one Hegar had drawn up that was costing Texas taxpayers millions.[53] States weren't the only ones doing the math: oil giant Chevron chose BlackRock to manage $8 billion of its 401(k) assets.[54]

When questioned about his critics, Larry Fink did not budge. "I believe stakeholder capitalism is not political. It is not woke. It is capitalism," he said.[55]

But the backlash clearly had an effect. As noted in chapter 1, Fink acknowledged in early 2023 that it had cost the firm $4 billion in assets under management.[56] His letter to investors that year equivocated about "the ultimate path and timing of the transition" of the energy economy, and he moved away from using the term "ESG," calling it "weaponized."[57]

Fink may not have been willing to admit that anything changed, but BlackRock's decision-making did. The firm took heat from climate advocates in the spring of 2022 after announcing it was likely to vote against climate-related shareholder proposals that were "more prescriptive or constraining on companies."[58] It also announced a "Voting Choice" program that would enable some retail clients to vote in proxy battles on questions such as climate strategy, thus increasing the voice of shareholders.[59] But the move that seemed most calculated to stall the political backlash in its tracks was the appointment of Amin Nasser, CEO of Saudi Aramco, the world's biggest oil company, to BlackRock's board in the summer of 2023.[60] It was suddenly hard to argue that

BlackRock was an agent of radical change out to destabilize the global economy.

The Other Side of the Coin

Political defenders of the fossil fuel industry weren't the only ones taking shots at BlackRock. Bluebell Capital Partners, an activist hedge fund that took a small position in the firm, raised concerns that it was "potentially fueling a gap between the 'talk' and the 'walk' on ESG investing" and that the political backlash it had sparked was impeding progress.[61]

Pressure for greater action on climate change extended beyond BlackRock. New York City's comptroller signaled to a number of financial firms through a series of shareholder resolutions that the city's pension funds wanted to see more concrete progress on climate change, or they would risk losing the city's business.[62] Legislators from several blue states took up bills that called for divestment of their state's pension funds from fossil fuels.[63] And multinationals had to reckon with political interests that went beyond red versus blue. BlackRock may have slowed its roll, but Norway's $1.4 trillion sovereign wealth fund said it would consider selling companies that made no progress on climate action.[64] Thousands of companies also faced the prospect of more demanding sustainability reporting rules from the European Union.[65]

The pressure from pro-ESG stakeholders mirrored broader concerns about accountability for ESG claims. In a letter to McDonald's shareholders, legendary activist investor Carl Icahn wrote, "A large number of Wall Street firms and their bankers and lawyers appear to be capitalizing on ESG to drive profits without doing nearly enough to support tangible societal progress."[66] Icahn framed his intentions in a way that would have made Milton Friedman roll over in his grave. By promoting change at leading corporations, Icahn wrote, "we can clean up insular boardrooms and drive lasting improvements for society as a whole."

The counter-backlash extended to *S*, or social, issues as well. As mentioned in chapter 1, California governor Gavin Newsom announced that the state would not renew a multimillion-dollar contract with

Walgreens after the pharmacy chain said it would not sell the abortion medication mifepristone in twenty-one states, including four in which abortion remained legal. "California will not stand by as corporations cave to extremists and cut off critical access to reproductive care and freedom," he said,[67] making it clear that the pressure on corporate leaders would come from both sides of the political spectrum.

5

DOERS, TALKERS, FENCE-SITTERS, AND STRADDLERS

Speaking out comes with a fundamental tension between impression management and accountability.[1] Business leaders who take stances generally want to be seen in a favorable light, whether they are trying to influence stakeholders or using their platforms to advance issues they care about personally. A disconnect between words and actions leads to a lack of legitimacy, which ultimately erodes trust in individuals and firms as well as in business as an institution.[2]

Accountability—defined here simply as doing what you say you will—begins with transparency, which enables third parties to verify a claim. Some researchers have made extensive efforts to track follow-through on CEO and corporate statements. The Plug, a digital news and insights company focused on the Black innovation economy, led a multiyear investigative report on tech companies' commitments to diversity, equity, and inclusion made in response to the murder of George Floyd. Its 2022 "State of the Pledge" report found that a lack of transparency made it difficult to gauge progress on many tech companies' commitments.[3] A McKinsey review of Fortune 1000 companies revealed that while 40 percent made statements in support of racial justice between May 2020 and October 2022, only 30 percent made external commitments to promote racial equity, and just 25 percent made internal commitments to promote diversity and inclusion.[4]

Such reports help the public make sense of what they hear from business leaders, and they put CEOs on notice that actions matter. Organizations such as Accountable.US and JUST Capital have created ranking systems that evaluate corporate performance on a range of measures, though neither directly link specific executive statements to actions.

But the impact of these efforts is limited because accountability ultimately rests in the eye of the stakeholder. If investors find a CEO's position on an issue sufficiently problematic, they can sell shares in that company. Customers can express their approval or disapproval through purchasing power or other measures of brand sentiment. Employee recruitment and retention can rise or fall based on a CEO's positions.

In other words, stakeholders make their own determinations about accountability, and these judgments coexist alongside all the other information they use to evaluate a firm. Researchers have constructed experiments that enable narrow measurements of how a CEO's position on a given issue affects the opinions of one group of stakeholders or another, but in real life, causality is ultimately difficult to disentangle, and the time horizon matters.

This distinction between talking and doing presumes that an executive has taken a stance on an issue. As mentioned in chapter 1, at times silence or following the crowd after others have acted are the best options. Both are forms of fence-sitting; the only difference is that followers ultimately hop off. Straddling, or trying to play both sides of the fence without falling off, is another approach that can succeed or fail depending on how skillfully it is done.

Doers and Talkers

Some leaders do outstanding jobs following through on what they say and making it easy for others to hold them accountable for that. One strong example was the response of Microsoft's Satya Nadella to the murder of George Floyd in 2020. Nadella addressed employees in a town hall shortly after Floyd's murder on May 25, and the CEO followed up initially with a firm-wide email on June 5 that previewed his thinking about a broad-based approach: "Each of us—starting with me and the senior leaders at the company—has a role to play. We cannot episodically wake up when a new tragedy occurs. A systemic problem requires a holistic response."[5]

Nadella noted existing long-standing initiatives to address racial inequity and pointed to six small initial commitments the company would make. Just as importantly, he referenced the firm's thirty-year-old employee resource group Blacks at Microsoft and said the corporate response would be "directly informed by the needs of the Black and African American community."

A couple weeks later, Nadella rolled out a more comprehensive set of steps Microsoft would take over the next five years in areas ranging from justice reform to representation within the company.[6] Some of the specifics included

- investing an additional $150 million in diversity and inclusion;
- doubling "the number of Black and African American people managers, senior individual contributors, and senior leaders" in its US workforce by 2025; and
- doubling "the number of Black- and African American–owned approved suppliers over the next three years" and spending "an incremental $500M with those existing and new suppliers."

He closed by grounding these actions in the needs that the moment revealed: "Employees expect this change from their leaders. Our customers and partners expect this change from Microsoft. And the world demands this change."

These commitments were clear and quantified, and, not surprisingly, Microsoft took a data-driven approach to sharing progress on them. Its 2022 *Global Diversity & Inclusion Report* (the latest as of this writing) provided a year-by-year breakdown of representation at the firm dating back to 2018, with detailed demographics for employees ranging from executives, partners, and directors to nontechnical and retail.[7] In June 2022, it also released a two-year snapshot of progress toward 2025 that showed the percentage accomplished toward specific goals such as the $500 million commitment to Black- and African American–owned suppliers.[8] While most of the numbers were impressive, Microsoft made no effort to hide its need for significant growth in hiring Hispanic and Latino leaders.

Advocates for racial equity or diversity might argue that Microsoft's goals were too modest for a firm that has topped $3 trillion in market

cap at its peak. But the goals Nadella did commit to were clearly articulated, systemic in nature, and responsive to input from the company's
employees. They were also easy to understand and trace. Executives
looking for an example of how to lead transparently on an urgent and
sensitive issue would be hard-pressed to find a better one.

✳

Wells Fargo was at the other end of the say-do continuum. Days after
the murder of George Floyd, CEO Charlie Scharf mentioned the 2019
Business Roundtable statement, which he signed right after moving
into the job. "I can commit that our company will do all we can to support our diverse communities and foster a company culture that deeply
values and respects diversity and inclusion," he said.[9]

A few weeks later, Scharf announced a list of commitments, including doubling Black leadership at the bank over the next five years.[10]
The other priorities were less specific, such as voluntary education and
mandatory training sessions, and evaluating senior leadership "based
upon their progress in improving diverse representation and inclusion
in their area of responsibility."

Scharf apparently found the goal of doubling Black leadership at
Wells Fargo harder than anticipated. In September 2020, he apologized after Reuters reported that he had written in an internal memo
that "while it might sound like an excuse, the unfortunate reality is that
there is a very limited pool of Black talent to recruit from." Scharf had
reiterated this point on a Zoom call with employees.[11] Sen. Elizabeth
Warren (D-MA) of the Senate Committee on Banking, Housing, and
Urban Affairs responded that Scharf's remarks revealed "an unfathom-
able blind spot."[12]

Eight months later, Wells Fargo was back in the headlines for all the
wrong reasons. Current and former employees of the bank said they
were directed to interview diverse candidates for jobs that had already
been promised to other applicants all to comply with an interviewing
policy established to increase diversity.[13]

These fake interviews sounded all too similar to a scandal that had
tarnished Wells Fargo's credibility since the mid-2010s: employees had
opened more than 2 million unauthorized customer accounts to boost

sales figures.[14] Shortly after Scharf took the reins, Wells Fargo finally settled that matter with the Justice Department for $3 billion.[15]

When the fake interviews came to light, Wells Fargo relied on the crisis communication playbook. In an unattributed statement, it first acknowledged the problem: "No one should be put through an interview without a real chance of receiving an offer, period." Then it announced a pause in its "diverse slate guidelines" that had led to the interviews.[16] If there was an opportunity to demonstrate leadership, Scharf let it pass.

Wells Fargo's July 2022 report on diversity, equity, and inclusion did not specifically mention progress toward Scharf's 2020 goal of doubling Black leadership within five years, though it charted a 3.1 percentage point increase in Black or African American executives between December 2020 (5.8 percent) and December 2021 (8.9 percent).[17] Clear traceability to the CEO's goals would have been a step in the direction of improving trust in its brand.

Big claims come with a greater need to show your homework. One of the headline-grabbing corporate responses to the murder of George Floyd was JPMorgan Chase's five-year, $30 billion commitment toward closing the racial wealth gap. CEO Jamie Dimon announced in October 2020: "We can do more and do better to break down systems that have propagated racism and widespread economic inequality, especially for Black and Latinx people. It's long past time that society addresses racial inequities in a more tangible, meaningful way."[18]

JPMorgan Chase had faced challenges with racism before the summer of 2020. A *New York Times* investigative report in December 2019 led five Democrats on the Senate Banking Committee to write Dimon a letter that called out the bank's "racist treatment of African American employees and customers," and questioned its commitment "to addressing systemic racism in banking and ensuring that it provides fair and equal access to financial services and opportunities to all."[19] Dimon's internal reply to the *Times* story said, "Racism has existed for too long—in our country, in our communities—and unfortunately, at times, even at our company. But this is not who we are."[20] He called for a review of policies, procedures, and practices but did not offer any specifics.

In his 2021 letter to shareholders, Dimon told a straightforward story of progress toward the $30 billion goal, reporting that the bank had already "deployed or committed" $18 billion by the end of that year.[21] *New York Times* reporter Emily Flitter did a deep dive into the commitment and found a more complex web of programs and initiatives that made it hard to determine what actually counted toward the total. "Some components of the pledge were presented entirely without numbers, time frames or any specifics," she concluded.[22] Other journalists raised related questions about the bank's transparency and its unwillingness to submit the pledge to an audit.[23]

JPMorgan Chase got less attention for a more targeted change in its hiring policies that was intended to help address barriers driven by systemic racism. In 2018 the bank "banned the box" asking about criminal or arrest records on job applications. Ban the box had been a priority for criminal justice reformers for years because of its disproportionate impact on communities of color.[24] In 2021 Dimon wrote in the *New York Times* that the bank had hired over two thousand new employees in 2020 with criminal backgrounds (roughly 10 percent of its total hires) as a result of this change, and he advocated for "clean slate" legislation that would accomplish more at scale.[25] In the grand scheme of addressing racial equity, it was a single piece of the puzzle that mostly created lower-wage jobs, but the progress it made was clear and measurable.

Fence-Sitters

On the eve of Disney's annual shareholder meeting in March 2022, CEO Bob Chapek was in a bind of his own making. The Florida state senate had just passed the Parental Rights in Education Act, which restricted what teachers could say about sexual orientation or gender identity.[26] This put the bill on the glide path to Governor Ron DeSantis's desk for his signature. LGBTQ+ advocates and allies had dubbed it the "Don't Say Gay" bill, and they pointed to data from the Centers for Disease Control and Prevention showing that LGBTQ+ youth face higher mental health risks than their peers and a lack of safety at school.[27]

With seventy-five thousand employees in Florida and its stature as one of the leading media and entertainment brands in the world, Disney had a powerful voice it could exercise.[28] And with thousands of LGBTQ+ employees in the United States (by a conservative estimate[29]), its response would extend far beyond its massive footprint in Orlando.

Chapek and Geoff Morrell, who joined Disney as its chief corporate affairs officer in January 2022, could have looked to two cases for precedent. The first was Bank of America's stance in 2016 when North Carolina took up a bill that restricted transgender peoples' use of public restrooms. Like Disney in Florida, Charlotte-based Bank of America was a major employer in its home state. CEO Brian Moynihan repeatedly spoke out unequivocally against the bill, offering two reasons for the decision: it was the right thing to do, and it addressed the concerns of the bank's employees. "We have teammates that, you know, it felt that that disenfranchised them and made them feel less, and so we had to pay attention," he said.[30]

The second was Delta Airlines' response to Georgia's restriction of voting rights in 2021. CEO Ed Bastian initially avoided taking a position that would pit the company against state lawmakers,[31] knowing the company would face economic retaliation. (Delta had already been down this road in 2018 when it ended a little-used discount for NRA members after the mass shooting at Marjory Stoneman Douglas High School.[32]) As the pressure mounted on Delta after seventy-plus Black business leaders led by Kenneth Chenault and Kenneth Frazier signed a letter calling on the business community to oppose the law, Bastian came out against it.[33] Georgia legislators promptly voted to withdraw a tax break that benefited Delta to the tune of $50 million.[34] It was the worst of both worlds: Bastian's long silence looked like unprincipled fence-sitting, and his final position came with a political sanction. Speaking out earlier would have demonstrated strong support for Delta's employees at no additional cost to the company. Months after the decision, Bastian said, "I think it's not possible to solely keep your head low, because if you keep your head low, that speaks also to people—not speaking."[35]

Compared to Delta's tax break, Disney had a lot at stake if it ran afoul of DeSantis. As part of the planning for Walt Disney World in the mid-1960s, the state had created an "independent special district" around the park that Disney could govern as its own municipality. DeSantis and Republican legislators could take away that autonomy as easily as the state had granted it decades earlier.

In the weeks before Disney's annual shareholder meeting, Chapek and Disney followed Bastian's initial approach. The company avoided taking a stance after the bill passed the Florida House of Representatives in February; that prompted Chapek's predecessor Bob Iger to post a tweet expressing his opposition to it.[36]

A few days before the state's Senate vote, the company had tried having it both ways: "We understand how important this issue is to our LGBTQ+ employees and many others. . . . The biggest impact we can have in creating a more inclusive world is through the inspiring content we produce, the welcoming culture we create here and the diverse organizations we support, including those representing the LGBTQ+ community."[37]

This empty-calories statement, however, demonstrated the opposite of what it said: the company did not understand how important the issue was to its employees.

Its position was not just one of conflicted ambivalence about politicizing the brand. Disney had already privately taken a stand with its checkbook. The *Orlando Sentinel* reported that Disney had given campaign donations to the sponsors or cosponsors of the bill.[38] (It later came out that the company had donated $125,000 to the Republican Party of Florida in January 2022, the same month the Don't Say Gay bill was introduced in the Florida House. Disney donated one-fifth of that amount to Florida Democrats in the same period.[39])

Two days before the shareholder meeting, Chapek rationalized his decision not to take a public position in an internal memo: "As we have seen time and again, corporate statements do very little to change outcomes or minds. Instead, they are often weaponized by one side or the other to further divide and inflame. Simply put, they can be counterproductive and undermine more effective ways to achieve change."[40]

But after the Senate vote, Chapek got off the fence, reversing course at the annual shareholder meeting. He began by recognizing that many people were upset with Disney's silence as the company tried to negotiate behind the scenes, and he admitted the outcome in Florida was "not what many of us were hoping for, especially our LGBTQ+ employees." He said Disney would join other companies in signing a Human

Rights Campaign letter and donating $5 million to protect LGBTQ+ rights. "I understand our original approach, no matter how well intended, didn't quite get the job done," he said.[41]

Chapek followed up with an internal memo to Disney employees, apologizing for the pain his silence had caused. "You needed me to be a stronger ally in the fight for equal rights and I let you down. I am sorry," he wrote.[42] He announced a pause in all political donations in Florida and an increase in support for advocacy groups. But for some, Chapek's contrition was too little, too late. In the weeks that followed, employees organized a Where Is Chapek website, accompanied by protests and walkouts.[43]

DeSantis and Florida's Republican legislators fired back predictably at Chapek's about-face. The following month, the governor signed a bill dissolving Disney's authority to self-govern the municipality around Walt Disney World.[44] This hasty act came loaded with a hefty price tag for homeowners in neighboring counties who would have to absorb over $1 billion in Disney's bond debt.[45] In February 2023, DeSantis signed a second bill that put the district under the control of a five-person board appointed by the governor and undid the first bill's mistake, which would have saddled nearby residents with years of massive tax increases.[46] Disney's eleventh-hour legal maneuvering effectively neutralized the power of the board,[47] but the public relations (PR) damage was done.

Morrell was out at Disney after less than four months.[48] Chapek may have thought that Morrell's Republican bona fides—he had worked in the Pentagon during the George W. Bush administration before spending a decade at oil giant BP[49]—would be useful in dealing with DeSantis. If so, Chapek miscalculated. DeSantis was waging a Viktor Orbán–style culture war. Nothing short of unswerving loyalty would appease him. "Woke Disney" fit perfectly into DeSantis's narrative about what was wrong with corporate America.[50]

Chapek weathered the PR storm in the short term, receiving a three-year contract extension from Disney's board at the end of June.[51] But by the late fall of 2022, after Disney fell far short of Wall Street estimates for revenue and earnings per share, Chapek was gone, and his predecessor Bob Iger was back as interim CEO.[52] The mishandling of the Don't Say Gay bill didn't kill Chapek's position, but it didn't help.

Florida governor Ron DeSantis retaliated against Disney because its CEO failed a loyalty test by publicly disagreeing with him.

Upon returning to Disney, Iger fought back more effectively than Chapek had. Disney sued DeSantis, accusing him of "a targeted campaign of government retaliation."[53] Iger reiterated the main message on an investor call: "This is about one thing and one thing only, and that's retaliating against us for taking a position about pending legislation. And we believe that in us taking that position, we were merely exercising our right to free speech."[54] A month later, shortly before DeSantis announced his candidacy for president, Disney canceled plans to build an office complex in Orlando that would have created two thousand new jobs.[55]

The free speech argument was the crux of the matter from the start. Corporations routinely take positions against pending legislation, either on their own or through trade associations. What was unique in this case was DeSantis's use of government power to punish Disney for doing so.

DeSantis doubled down on the Parental Rights in Education Act by signing a follow-on bill in 2023 that proscribed the language that can be used to teach sexual education to all Florida students in grades K–12.[56] As he campaigned for president, he began accusing Disney of "sexualizing children"[57]—a charge that had nothing to do with the company's disagreement with the Parental Rights in Education Act.

The impact on Disney's brand was not clear from the data. The Axios Harris annual surveys of the top hundred US brands showed that Disney slipped from number 5 in 2019 to 77 in 2023,[58] but a closer look reveals a more nuanced story. Disney's slide began in 2020 (number 22) and continued in 2021 (number 37), before it fell to number 65 in 2022 when the controversy flared.[59] Poll results are just one measure of a brand's strength, and different questions yield different answers. In March 2022 when Chapek broke his silence, Global Strategy Group's "Business & Politics Annual Study" recorded Disney's approval rating at 74 percent, which was no different than it was two years earlier at the beginning of the pandemic.[60] (Similar to the Axios Harris findings, Global Strategy Group's poll tracked a decline for Disney from 2019 to 2020.)

Financial data also provided perspective on DeSantis's efforts to tarnish the company's image. In the second quarter of 2023, its US theme parks raked in 50 percent more operating income than they had in pre-pandemic 2019,[61] suggesting that plenty of American families still trusted the Disney brand.

✳

Sometimes fence-sitting is a temporary move, a matter of wanting to follow rather than lead the pack. This tactic was apparent with the sudden and immense pressure on multinational corporations to exit Russia after Vladimir Putin's invasion of Ukraine on February 24, 2022. It posed a stark and immediate test that transcended America's domestic culture wars or debates about ESG. The Friedmanite argument for profits over politics ran smack into both the reputational risk of being on the wrong side of history and the political risks of remaining in business with Putin, to say nothing of the moral questions.

Four days after the invasion, Jeffrey Sonnenfeld of the Chief Executive Leadership Institute at the Yale School of Management led an interdisciplinary team of dozens of experts that began tracking companies that were suspending or ending operations in Russia.[62] Within two weeks, hundreds of companies had begun to act, and within two months the number had grown to nearly a thousand companies.[63] The list graded companies on a scale from A to F depending on the extent of their withdrawal from Russia. (As of the spring of 2023, it is still being updated continuously.)

Sonnenfeld viewed the list as a tool that could help CEOs make the call. "The CEOs who had courage to step out in front often inspire the not-so-courageous CEOs, or the ones who don't have the support of their boards," said Sonnenfeld. "So they do what people in the business jargon world would call 'the benchmarking.' They want peer affirmation. So [by] putting out the good guys list, they can see there's a thundering herd there of people moving with you—don't worry."[64]

Not everyone sat on the fence. Brian Chesky of Airbnb announced both a suspension of operations in Russia and Belarus, and a plan to provide housing for up to 100,000 Ukrainian refugees.[65] "The moment this huge refugee crisis occurred, we asked, 'How can we help?' and the answer is to provide housing to as many people as possible," he said.[66]

Executive teams and boards may have fretted privately about financial losses, but they dared not voice these concerns in public while Ukrainians faced unspeakable horrors. Shell's CEO apologized for buying Russian oil. "We are acutely aware that our decision last week to purchase a cargo of Russian crude oil to be refined into products like petrol and diesel—despite being made with security of supplies at the forefront of our thinking—was not the right one and we are sorry," said CEO Ben van Beurden.[67] His statement wasn't dismissed as woke posturing.

Exiting Russia came with undeniable costs for capital-intensive businesses. But Sonnenfeld and his team found in the first three months after the invasion that markets significantly rewarded companies that left Russia, even those that took a one-time loss.[68] The companies' judgments were ultimately about risk, not morality. "Capital allocators clearly and unequivocally believe the risks associated with remaining in Russia at a time when nearly 1,000 major global corporations have exited far outweigh the costs of exiting Russia," Sonnenfeld and his colleagues concluded. Doing the right thing was good for business.

It would prove more difficult for some businesses than others to get out of Russia. BP was one of the first firms to announce its intention to exit. "It has caused us to fundamentally rethink bp's position with Rosneft," said CEO Bernard Looney just days after the invasion of Ukraine. "I am convinced that the decisions we have taken as a board are not only the right thing to do, but are also in the long-term interests of bp."[69] Months later, as the company struggled to sell its stake in Russia's state-owned Rosneft, it emphasized there was no disconnect between its words and actions, as it was neither operating in nor profiting from Russia. "bp has no intention of returning to business as usual in Russia," the firm stated in December. "It was anticipated that this would be—and it is proving to be—a drawn-out process."[70] The announcement was a nonevent for the markets, which had already priced in the costs and benefits of the company's position.

Straddling

Russia's invasion of Ukraine posed a particularly difficult challenge for Western pharmaceutical companies. While international humanitarian law dating back to the Geneva Conventions protects access to medication in times of war,[71] these companies had to decide how to serve Russians needing medications while their government inflicted suffering on millions of Ukrainians.

Pfizer found a way to engage that might be characterized as smart straddling. Its solution, which it announced in a statement, was to honor its value of putting patients first by maintaining humanitarian supplies of medicines in Russia while donating all proceeds to direct humanitarian support in Ukraine.[72] Pfizer made clear that maintaining this supply of medicines did not mean continuing business as usual in Russia, and it outlined specific activities it would discontinue, such as not initiating new clinical trials within the country.

"We preserved our principle of putting the patient first while also making clear that we opposed Russian aggression," wrote chief corporate affairs officer Sally Susman.[73]

✳

A different type of straddling is trying not to offend anyone. Anheuser-Busch took this approach when responding to social media attacks on Bud Light for its marketing relationship with transgender influencer Dylan Mulvaney. In April 2023, shortly after Mulvaney shared an Instagram video featuring a customized can of Bud Light with her image on it, anti-LGBTQ+ conservatives voiced outrage on social media and called for a boycott of the brand. Kid Rock, a Michigan native who used to perform in front of a backdrop of the Confederate flag, appeared in a video shooting up cases of Bud Light with an assault rifle and reeling off a string of expletives.[74]

The activists behind this campaign made no secret of their intentions. Matt Walsh posted the game plan to his 2 million–plus followers at the time on Twitter: "Here's what we should do: Pick a victim, gang up on it, and make an example of it. We can't boycott every woke company or even most of them. But we can pick one, it hardly matters which, and target it with a ruthless boycott campaign. Claim one scalp then move on to the next."[75]

Even before the boycott, Bud Light faced several challenges that made its position as America's number 1 beer tenuous. Its sales were in long-term decline, mirroring the downward trend for beer relative to

spirits.[76] It also had recently raised its prices weeks before the controversy flared.[77] Finally, customers had plenty of alternatives (substitute
goods) that they could choose instead.

Anheuser-Busch's leaders had two sets of considerations to weigh:
evidence and ethics. In a divided country, consumer brands built on
mass appeal such as Bud Light or Coke require different strategies than
those that cultivate a clear cultural identity such as Ben & Jerry's or
Black Rifle Coffee.

Beyond what Anheuser-Busch knew internally from its customer
data, the evidence was challenging. When opinions on a social or political issue are highly polarized, research shows that the average response to a firm's stance on that issue is negative.[78] Sadly, support for
transgender people is highly polarized: a 2022 poll from the Pew Research Center found the public evenly divided on whether acceptance
of transgender people has gone too far (38 percent) or not far enough
(36 percent).[79] With Bud Light, anti-LGBTQ+ activists tapped into this
polarization. While the controversy they stoked stemmed from a marketing effort rather than a position statement from the company, the
net response from consumers was largely the same. And as noted in
chapter 1, more people are inclined to say, "Cancel my subscription"
than "sign me up" in response to a position.[80]

On the ethical side, the activists positioned themselves as aggrieved
by Bud Light's recognition of a trans person. As self-appointed social
gatekeepers, their verdict boiled down to "not one of us." The principled way to respond to this message of exclusion would be to double
down on respect and appreciation for beer drinkers from all walks of
life, not just those approved by one corner of Twitter.

The evidence and the ethics didn't offer easy answers, but they
pointed to two coherent strategies. First, there was a sound rationale
for maintaining disciplined silence and waiting out the storm since
many consumer boycotts tend to lose steam. The argument for silence
was that anything the company said could be weaponized and potentially prolong the story. The challenge with silence was that it provided
zero opportunity to shape the narrative. And if the boycott gained mo-
mentum, the pressure to do something would grow.

The other option, releasing a clear statement that "Bud Light is for
everyone who enjoys a beer that's easy to drink," would send a positive,

DOERS, TALKERS, FENCE-SITTERS, AND STRADDLERS   69

live-and-let-live message to the average customer who just wanted to crack open a cold one at the end of the day without getting bogged down in politics. It would also reframe the matter in terms of personal freedom. The risk in this approach was implicit in the rationale for silence: anything the company said might feed the story rather than neutralize it.

Either of these options also could have been complemented by a hurry-up offense of marketing activity designed to create a diversion.

The company started by saying nothing. But after nearly two weeks, when the story showed no sign of dying down, silence gave way to straddling when Anheuser-Busch CEO Brendan Whitworth issued a long statement on Twitter.[81] Its moral substance—"We never intended to be part of a discussion that divides people"—sounded more like an apology for offending Kid Rock than an affirmation of what the brand stood for. It signaled weakness rather than strength, leaving nobody satisfied and adding fuel to the fire.

The case for offering a principled response came later in the spring from the CEO of Target, which also faced an anti-LGBTQ+ backlash for carrying Pride month–themed clothing. After customer outbursts, the company took flak for removing some of these items in selected stores because of its concerns about worker safety, and CEO Brian Cornell addressed the criticism.[82] He sent an email to Target employees expressing appreciation for their perseverance and professionalism under difficult circumstances, and he wrote directly "to the LGBTQIA+ community": "One of the hardest parts in all of this was trying to contemplate how the adjustments we're making to alleviate these threats to our team's physical and psychological safety would impact you and your wellbeing and psychological safety. We stand with you now and will continue to do so—not just during Pride Month, but each and every day."

Two months into the boycott, with sales down 24 percent, Bud Light lost its decades-long position as the best-selling beer in America.[83] Anheuser-Busch announced a marketing pivot, featuring new ads focused on the people behind its beers such as drivers and farmers.[84] This could have been part of a strong feature of a proactive, apolitical counternarrative from the start.

It is hard to imagine that Anheuser-Busch would have fared worse if it had voiced the courage of its convictions rather than straddling. The drop in Bud Light sales significantly cut into the company's second-quarter (Q2) North American revenue, but the damage to the brand appeared limited to a vocal minority: the company reported on its Q2 earnings call that eight in ten consumers surveyed (80 percent) had favorable or neutral opinions of Bud Light.[85] It also found that customers wanted "to enjoy their beer without a debate," a sentiment it could have promoted with a "Bud Light is for everyone" message.

After making no comment for nearly three months, Dylan Mulvaney called out the company for its response, noting that it never contacted her and that she faced "more bullying and transphobia than I could have ever imagined."[86] In response, Anheuser-Busch turned to the crisis communications playbook, with a spokesperson emailing a generic statement: "The privacy and safety of our employees and our partners is always our top priority."

Part II

NEW RULES

6

LISTEN FIRST

Speaking out can inspire fear because of the risk of coming across as insensitive or out of touch. There is no question this can happen, as illustrated with the example of Charlie Scharf of Wells Fargo attributing the bank's difficulties in hiring Black leaders to a scarcity of talent in the pipeline (see chapter 5).[1] Many executives view racial issues in particular as a trip wire: Edelman found that six in ten (61 percent) are uncomfortable discussing race with people of other races for fear that they will accidentally say something racist.[2]

The first step toward being a more skillful communicator about any emotionally charged subject is for leaders to listen before they speak. It sounds like Corporate Communications 101—because it is—but plenty of leaders still fail to do it.

One enduring reason why is the inverse relationship between power and empathy.[3] Social scientists have validated something that prophets and playwrights have understood for millennia: power can lead to a reduced ability to understand how others think or feel.[4] Even when powerful people do listen, they are not always inclined to take the advice of others, regardless of their advisers' expertise.[5] This helps to explain why many firms increasingly value skills associated with emotional intelligence such as "theory of mind"—the ability to put oneself in another's shoes—when hiring CEOs.[6]

Investors

Where stakeholders are concerned, *power, legitimacy,* and *urgency* shape the listening priorities of CEOs.[7] Investors are the VIP frequent flyers who don't wait in line to be heard, and good CEOs proactively manage communication with their biggest investors. Size matters, though smaller investors can find ways to punch above their weight, as Bluebell Capital Partners demonstrated with its critique of Black-Rock's action on climate change.[8] Whether through private meetings, earnings calls, or shareholder proposals, investors have no shortage of opportunities to air their views, even if they aren't always happy with the answers they get.

Depending on an investor's philosophy and time horizon, reactions to a stance on a social or political issue can run the gamut from vehement objections to fervent support. As noted in chapter 2, Tim Cook and Howard Schultz knew they could dismiss shareholder proposals by conservative activists intent on scoring political points because the returns they achieved gave them leverage. In a start-up context, the dynamics can be reversed. "If you have all these predatory shareholders, they can very much influence the messaging for your company," said Dr. Paul Y. Song, CEO of NKGen Biotech.[9]

Customers

Efforts to understand customer sentiment can take place on multiple levels, depending on whether a business is a business-to-business (B2B) or business-to-consumer (B2C) company and whether it is product- or service-based. Personal relationships are the coin of the realm in high-touch, knowledge-based sectors such as consulting, law, or investment banking, while everyone is equally anonymous at a gas station. Fortunately, companies can draw on an entire industry dedicated to understanding the "voice of the customer" through a range of tools. Social media can play a part by allowing customers to register their enthusiasm or displeasure in the town square or to band together around common concerns or interests. The downside, of course, is that it can overamplify the views of a small number of very loud voices, as noted in the discussion of Bud Light and Target in chapter 5.[10] While social media is not without risks, it also provides an opportunity for forward-thinking companies and executives to listen and engage proactively.

For a large corporation with a broad customer base, trying to divine sentiments about political or social issues is an exercise in slicing and dicing its customers based on geography, age, income, and a host of other measures. It may not be possible to listen in the aggregate, but the next best thing in highly polarized times is being able to make informed decisions about the size and relative importance of various customer segments. It's one thing for a business to have an idea of how an issue is likely to play among millennials and Gen Zers versus retirees, and it's another to overlay that with the knowledge that three-quarters of its customers are younger than fifty years old. (See chapter 10 for more on segmenting customers.)

Employees

Where the workforce is concerned, the pendulum has swung strongly in the direction of management's seeking to understand the concerns and interests of employees on pressing issues that affect their lives. This is dramatically different from the days when communication flowed from the top down and when command-and-control leadership was the norm rather than the exception. Several factors may have contributed to this, including a generational shift in norms, the changes driven by tech culture that flattened hierarchies, and the competition for talent in boom times that gave employees more leverage with management than in the past.[11] This last argument is offset somewhat by Edelman's finding that employees who are *less* secure in their employment (66 percent) are more likely than those who feel secure in their jobs over the next year (59 percent) to expect their CEOs to speak out about issues that matter to them.[12]

Whatever the reasons, the importance of listening to employees is paramount. In many cases, employees are the driving force behind CEOs' decisions to speak out. When American Airlines announced that it opposed a restrictive voting bill in Texas in April 2021,[13] it was the result of what then-CEO Doug Parker was hearing from employees. "We did it in support of our team. I was getting emails and reach-out from a number of our Black employees in Texas letting me know this was really concerning to them, and they'd seen other companies speak up, [and] wanted to know what we were going to do," Parker said.[14]

Listening to learn from employees requires different skills than the ones used when listening to make decisions about business problems. This is doubly true with matters intrinsically connected to personal identity, such as those around diversity and inclusion. "You have to

Listening to learn from employees requires different skills than the ones used when listening to make decisions about business problems.

have this ability not just to communicate out but to listen in," said Mark Tercek, former CEO of the Nature Conservancy. "With a lot of people, you don't know how they're feeling."[15]

Tercek's insight speaks to the importance of adopting a posture of cultural humility, which can be thought of as an awareness of both power imbalances and the limitations of one's own perspective.[16] It means embracing the realization that "you don't know what you don't know" and that tone matters. There's a world of difference, for instance, between saying, "I understand how difficult that must be," and "that sounds really difficult."

Employee Resource Groups

In large organizations, one way that leaders can bridge this gap is through collaborating with employee resource groups (ERGs). Ever since Black employees at Xerox organized a group in the mid-1960s, ERGs have provided a forum for employees from underrepresented or marginalized groups to discuss issues that matter to them, including diversity and inclusion challenges within their organizations as well as broader societal concerns.[17] ERGs centered on women, LGBTQ+, and race or ethnicity are among the most common.[18]

On social issues ranging from voting rights to public restroom access to abortion, ERGs can serve as a source of knowledge and perspective for leaders seeking to understand issues outside their lived experience. "Sometimes the best participation and engagement an executive can have is to just sit and listen," said Michelle Rodriguez, the director of diversity, inclusion, and belonging at LinkedIn.[19]

LinkedIn has a robust ERG ecosystem, with eight thousand of its twenty-one thousand employees participating in ten global groups that the organization supports and funds. Each of the groups has two global leaders, who have significant visibility with the firm's CEO and top executives.

Where speaking out is concerned, one way that LinkedIn's ERGs serve their members and strengthen the company is by aligning what the company says publicly with the experience of employees on the inside. "The way we talk about things externally has to match how we're doing things internally," said Rodriguez. "Employees don't want to go to the LinkedIn platform and see a splashy effort to be very socially just and inclusive and then not feel it on the inside."

As a result, ERGs sometimes review statements, campaigns, and other public-facing communications on social issues before they go public. "It's created a way for our ERGs to feel like they have a strategic voice," Rodriguez said. "This elevates their role in a very meaningful way."

Many companies have ERGs, but the extent to which they are supported varies widely. "ERGs aren't real until you fund them," said Eleanor Lacey, the general counsel for Asana, which has six ERGs that it funds for its thousand-plus employees.[20] "Otherwise they're affinity groups."

When talking about racism and racial injustice, most employees value ERGs. Edelman found that two-thirds expect their employers to convene conversations about racism and DEI in the workplace (65 percent) and to maintain ERGs or affinity groups (68 percent).[21]

The Merits and Limitations of Listening

While ERGs can be powerful tools for listening to and collaborating with employees, some CEOs rely on other methods of keeping their fingers on the pulse. "If I have to wait for an ERG to have a meeting, shame on me. I have to have my ear to the ground. I have to have such a relationship with not just my senior leadership, but all these other individuals who feel comfortable reaching out to me directly. That's when you really hear what's happening," said Dana Maiman, CEO of IPG Health.[22]

The murder of George Floyd brought the importance of listening front and center for many leaders. "We spent time with our employees, listening. Because this is just painful. And what came of that was that there was a feeling of connection, a feeling of 'I don't have the lived experience of an African American, but I do want to understand that pain, that fear when somebody tells me they can't have their 12-year-old son go out and ride his bike,'" said Beth Ford, CEO of Land O' Lakes.[23]

For Dana Maiman, it was a reminder that her company's efforts had to continue. "When George Floyd happened, that wasn't a catalyst for us to start prioritizing DE&I. It just further reinforced why we needed to keep doing what we're doing with our commitment to all of those principles," she said. "This was an instance where we really opened it up to so many of our employees. I need their voices."[24]

There are limits to what listening can accomplish. Absent any follow-through, it leads to frustration. And with speaking out, just as with other decisions, leaders ultimately have to make hard calls that will leave some people unhappy. "When people come wanting the CEO to speak out, most of the time the answer is no," said Michelle Rodriguez.[25]

Listening is not a cure-all, but failing to listen can lead to errors that have costly consequences for one's credibility and legitimacy.

Key Insights: Listening First

Listening first is about adopting a mindset, not just a behavior.

1. *Mind the gap between power and empathy.* Just as politicians often don't know the price their constituents pay for a gallon of milk, chief executives run the same risk of being out of touch with the concerns and interests of the very people they are expected to understand and support. Good leaders are aware of this gap and find meaningful ways to stay connected with people who keep them grounded in the realities outside their bubble.

2. *Distinguish between two modes of listening.* Listening to learn is fundamentally about seeking to understand another person's perspective. It is not the same as listening to gather information for a decision. Doing it effectively requires a combination of humility and emotional intelligence. Sometimes simply listening is the best answer.

3. *Invest the time.* Listening well is an act of respect. It does not imply concurrence or agreement. The ability to validate emotions, to acknowledge substantive differences without dismissing them, and to respond with both clarity and humanity is a practice that cannot be rushed. Done well, it fosters mutual respect and admiration.

7

LIVED EXPERIENCE MATTERS

In October 2014, Apple CEO Tim Cook penned an opinion piece for Bloomberg confirming speculation about his personal life that had circulated widely for years.[1] "Plenty of colleagues at Apple know I'm gay," he wrote in the third paragraph.[2] And with that characteristically understated disclosure, Cook became the first openly gay CEO of a Fortune 500 company.[3]

But before getting to what he wanted to share, he explained why he was speaking out at that point, a few years into his tenure as CEO. Citing what Dr. Martin Luther King called life's most persistent and urgent question—"What are you doing for others?"—Cook acknowledged, "My desire for personal privacy has been holding me back from doing something more important."

That "something more important" was using his voice to help others. After noting both his own extraordinary privilege and the discrimination that many still face because of their sexual orientation, he made the case for speaking out: "So if hearing that the CEO of Apple is gay can help someone struggling to come to terms with who he or she is, or bring comfort to anyone who feels alone, or inspire people to insist on their equality, then it's worth the trade-off with my own privacy." He framed this in the context of giving back to those who had paved the way for his own relative comfort in life as an openly gay man. "I don't consider myself an activist, but I realize how much I've benefited from the sacrifice of others."

Cook's announcement combined humility, empathy, and self-awareness with a commitment to action. He trumpeted his company's support for legislation promoting workplace equality and marriage equality, as well as its efforts to oppose a discriminatory bill in Arizona. "I will personally continue to advocate for equality for all people until my toes point up," he wrote, using a phrase that has become his go-to for signaling determination to stay the course on public policy issues.

To Silicon Valley insiders and business journalists, Cook's Bloomberg piece may have been a ho-hum affair revealing nothing more than an open secret. After all, a CNBC journalist had mistakenly outed him on live television just months before.[4] Three years earlier, *Out* magazine had ranked him first on its list of the fifty most powerful gay and lesbian people in America.[5] But regardless of the dynamics around Cook's timing, his message stands a decade later as an example of how an executive can use a platform to reach an audience that feels unheard.

Walking the Line between Public and Private

A personal perspective is a different mode of persuasion than a reasoned argument. Like a story, it enables an audience to empathize with the speaker, to imagine what it is like to see the world from that point of view. By sharing something deeply personal, Tim Cook allowed readers to consider the questions and concerns that he had balanced in private for years before deciding to go public. He also established himself as someone who understands what LGBTQ+ freedom means to a person's life.

On one level it's common sense that lived experience matters when weighing in on certain issues. A person from any group that faces marginalization, discrimination, or exclusion knows it differently than the best-intended ally who lacks a firsthand perspective. Experience bolsters credibility, just as it does for someone who has served in a war, cared for the sick, or given birth to a child. That much is intuitive.

But in the bigger picture, the trend toward CEOs speaking about lived experience represents a dramatic shift away from a more impersonal style that was still the norm at the turn of the twenty-first century. Today the line between one's public and private life is much thinner.

The contrast between Cook and his old boss Steve Jobs is instructive. Jobs gave countless interviews in Apple's early days and again after he returned to lead the company in the mid-1990s, but it's hard to imagine him using his own story to discuss social issues that could affect the company, such as immigration policy. As he said in 1994,

The trend toward CEOs speaking about lived experience represents a dramatic shift away from a more impersonal style that was the norm at the turn of the twenty-first century.

"When one is somewhat in the public eye, it's very important to keep a private life."[6]

A quarter century later, Cook drew on Jobs's legacy in a statement opposing Donald Trump's ban on immigrants from seven primarily Muslim countries in 2017, noting that Jobs was the biological son of a Syrian immigrant: "Steve was the son of an immigrant. Our company has immigrants in it that are key to the innovation of our company."[7] Nobody would accuse Cook of being an oversharer, but taken together, these examples show that he melded the personal and professional in his communication in a way that the more charismatic Jobs did not.

Speaking from personal experience doesn't have to involve a heavy privacy trade-off. Microsoft CEO Satya Nadella didn't reveal any new information about his life when he invoked his perspective as an immigrant in a statement condemning Trump's immigration policy that separated children from their parents at the border.[8] Instead, he alluded to the American dream: "I consider myself a product of two amazing and uniquely American things—American technology reaching me where I was growing up that allowed me to dream the dream and an enlightened immigration policy that then allowed me to live that dream. My story would not have been possible anywhere else."

In contrasting the approach to immigration that helped enable his success in achieving that dream, he called the Trump policy "abusive and cruel." Nadella also linked his remarks to a detailed statement by Microsoft president Brad Smith, who advocated for specific actions by the US government to reform the immigration system.[9]

Carol Tomé, CEO of UPS, talked about how her lived experience as a farmer informs her views on the environment. "From a climate perspective, I think I'm maybe more sensitive than some because I actually grow crops. I grow corn and wheat and soybeans. So I have some sensitivity to what a warmer planet means."[10] This quick snapshot of her life outside the office demonstrated the "show, don't tell" technique without delving into any personal details.

Tackling Taboos

At the other end of the spectrum, some executives have fewer concerns about privacy and use their platforms to dismantle the notion of the superhuman CEO or entrepreneur. "That might mean talking about the fact that I'm queer, that might mean talking about the fact that I'm an immigrant or that might mean talking about my struggles and mental health," Emma McIlroy, cofounder and chief executive of women's fashion company Wildfang, told *Forbes*.[11] McIlroy, who previously worked for Nike, sought to normalize discussions of mental health among entrepreneurs. "Somehow, mental health challenges are seen as a weakness or something to feel guilty or ashamed about, even though so many people are affected. The only way we're going to remove the taboo is by talking about it."

McIlroy's example is a reminder that CEOs don't need a global platform like Tim Cook's to speak powerfully from personal experience. Many leaders of purpose-driven businesses have a direct connection to their company's mission, and this enables them to express shared concerns or interests to their customers, employees, or investors.

McIlroy is one of a growing number of business leaders who have been candid about mental health challenges in recent years. EarnUp cofounder Matthew Cooper announced in December 2020 that he was stepping down as a CEO because of ongoing mental health challenges. He emphasized that he was going public about it to help break down barriers. "While nearly half the population will experience mental illness in their lifetime, we still live in a culture that generally keeps discussions about mental illness in the shadows. This silence is rampant across many areas of society, but corporate life maintains a particular type of secrecy and shame around the topic," he wrote.[12]

Karen Lynch, CEO of CVS, spoke about how she wrestled for years with the stigma associated with mental illness. "At twelve years old, my mom died by suicide, and I wouldn't talk about it for decades," she said. "And people need to talk about it because that's how people are going to get the access and the help that they need."[13]

Amy Gilliland, president of General Dynamics Information Technology, made a similar point after a company employee died by suicide. In a sector in which keeping secrets is an inherent part of the job, she noted that silence perpetuates the problem. "The most important thing for people to feel empowered to come forward and say they're not okay is to remove the stigma of mental health," she said in a prime-time television interview.[14]

While this kind of openness is still the exception rather than the norm, the pandemic drove many leaders to connect in new ways. Charles Lowrey, president and CEO of Prudential Financial, made weekly recordings on his iPhone that went out to the company's workforce. "I talked about my feelings," he said. "Leading during a crisis means a combination of strong leadership on one hand, but also incredibly empathetic and potentially vulnerable leadership on the other hand. Because people wanted to know you were feeling the same thing they were."[15]

Thasunda Brown Duckett, president and CEO of TIAA, was frank about her own anguish after the murder of George Floyd. "I feel it's important to acknowledge the anger, fear, hurt and uncertainty we are feeling," she wrote on LinkedIn.[16] "Like many of you, I am not O.K. I am still processing my pain." She also drew the connection between her own perspective at that moment and the forces of structural racism that perpetuate injustice in the United States. "We need to shine a light on this pain."

Shared Stories

Lived experience can also represent a collective sense of struggle, as it did for the group of seventy-two Black executives who signed a letter in the spring of 2021 challenging other corporate leaders to condemn Republicans' efforts to suppress voting in many states. The letter appeared days after Georgia Republicans responded to the defeat of both incumbent Republican U.S. senators and Donald Trump's loss of the state to Joe Biden in 2020 by passing a law that increased voting restrictions.[17]

Kenneth Chenault, former CEO of American Express and one of the letter's organizers, put the issue in historical terms. "Many people died for the right of Blacks being able to vote," he told CNN Business.[18]

Kenneth Frazier, former CEO of Merck and co-organizer of the letter, explained, "As African-American business executives, we don't have the luxury of being bystanders to injustice."[19] He also cited the inaction by other corporate leaders as a motivation for writing the letter. "There seems to be no one speaking out," Frazier told the *New York Times*.

Chenault and Frazier, both born before the passage of the Civil Rights Act and the Voting Rights Act, grew up in a time when the suppression of Black voters was a given in much of the country. As leaders who came of age as the United States became more democratic, their voices carried weight as living witnesses to that history.

Group letters are often bland statements, but this one, which appeared as a two-page spread in the *New York Times* and the *Washington Post*, did not mince words: "As Black business leaders, we cannot sit silently in the face of this gathering threat to our nation's democratic values and allow the fundamental right of Americans, to cast their votes for whomever they choose, to be trampled upon yet again."[20] Their ask was clear: "Corporate America should publicly oppose any discriminatory legislation and all measures designed to limit Americans' ability to vote."

Within a day of the letter's publication, Delta Airlines and Coca-Cola, two of Georgia's largest employers, both condemned the law; neither had done so previously.[21] Delta CEO Ed Bastian also spoke with Chenault before writing an internal memo that called the law "unacceptable" and out of step with the company's values.

These statements did nothing to change the law. They lacked the financial impact of Major League Baseball's decision to move the All-Star Game from Atlanta to Denver in response to the law, potentially costing the state up to $60 million.[22] But Chenault, Frazier, and their cosignatories put the rest of corporate America on notice: the attacks on democracy that threatened to disenfranchise Black Americans could not go ignored.

Key Insights: Speaking from Lived Experience

While some leaders are reluctant to talk about their own experience for fear of seeming self-centered, the examples shared in this chapter show how it can be done gracefully.

1. *Explain why.* Setting the context for a personal story gives you the opportunity to define your intentions. Tim Cook prefaced the substance of his piece by defining the tension he experienced between maintaining his privacy and doing something important, and he provided his rationale for speaking out—to help, bring comfort, and inspire. Emma McIlroy put it bluntly: "I lived through enough of those really dark, crappy moments myself that I'm passionate about trying to figure out how anybody else going through them doesn't have to go as dark and as low."[23]

2. *Establish an emotional connection.* The advantage of sharing based on personal experience is the ability to persuade through emotion rather than logic or cost-benefit analysis. A leader's story can connect with an audience in a way that opens the door to empathy. It doesn't take much: Satya Nadella created a simple image of himself growing up in India with a dream. A visual image helps to elicit an emotional response from an audience. As my friend Sally Kohn says, "When in doubt, be human."

3. *Link to values.* A perspective based on lived experience is most powerful when it serves as a point of entry to a bigger picture. The letter that seventy-two Black executives signed in response to the Georgia voter suppression law connected the right to vote both to American ideals and to the memory of those who have sacrificed to uphold them. Lived experience is bounded by the context of a specific moment in time; values endure.

4. *Clarify what's at stake.* The purpose for offering a personal perspective should be clear. The letter signed by Black leaders was unambiguous about the challenge it sought to address: "The fundamental tenets of our democracy are under assault."[24] That kind of clarity eliminates any potential confusion about a speaker's intentions.

5. *Connect to action.* Speaking from lived experience is of limited value if it doesn't lead to action. Tim Cook highlighted Apple's efforts to support LGBTQ+ equality in several states, and Satya Nadella coordinated his remarks about immigration with a detailed call for action by Microsoft president Brad Smith. There is no better way to ensure that a truth shared from lived experience won't be dismissed as spin.

8

VALUES MATTER

In a dynamic world in which issues constantly arise and recede, values can be a stabilizing force that helps to guide decisions about speaking out.

Critics often dismiss any mention of values by business leaders as "virtue signaling." The reality is that corporations and their executives have been virtue signaling for decades. At the height of World War II, companies such as IBM and Westinghouse bought ads in *Life* magazine exhorting Americans to defend democracy and support the war effort.[1] Sixty years later, when former Starbucks CEO Jim Donald praised American military personnel fighting overseas in December 2004, nobody accused him of virtue signaling.[2] Every corporate reminder to "support our troops" has been a loud and clear nod to the virtue of patriotism. There is nothing inherently right or wrong or liberal or conservative about virtue signaling. The fact that it is used as a putdown by current-day culture warriors opposed to one issue or another doesn't change that.

Corporate values statements may strike some as feel-good wallpaper, but they play a vital function when a firm needs to remind itself and others what it stands for. The linkage between shared values and the creation of a culture of excellence has been understood for decades, as has the connection between values and strategic decision-making.[3]

In multinational firms, cultural and linguistic differences complicate conversations about shared values. A misalignment between the values handed down from a company's headquarters and those of its foreign subsidiaries can lead to a diminished sense of commitment in the field, particularly if there is a perceived gap between what HQ says and what it does.[4] This only reinforces the importance both of developing or modifying corporate values through a transparent, consultative process and of aligning words and deeds. (See chapter 9, "Values Are Not Enough.")

When considering whether to engage on an issue, values offer a lens that can help clarify what's in scope for a firm. "For me, it's letting our values guide our actions. Those values include respect, responsibility, integrity," said Carol Tomé, CEO of UPS. "So it's letting our values guide our actions, and where we need to have a stronger voice, we'll have one based on our values. And where we don't, we won't."[5]

Values can also offer an ex post rationale for a position. "You can justify it [a stance] on just doing what's right if you need to," said Doug Parker, former CEO of American Airlines, noting that a leader might provide multiple reasons to explain why an issue merits attention.[6]

Four Dimensions That Connect Values and Culture

But values don't guide leaders' decisions in a vacuum. They are inextricably linked to a firm's employees and culture. Values help people determine if they fit in with an organization.[7] A content analysis of values statements from several hundred firms found that values speak to four dimensions of an organization's culture: *involvement, consistency, adaptability,* and *mission.*[8] Where considerations about speaking out are concerned, this suggests that values can shed light from the following multiple angles.

Involvement: Strengthening Employee Engagement

Values are part of a company's attractiveness to employees. "In the old days you'd just go to work for a company. Now you want to work for a company that shares your values, and one that you can be proud of," said Dana Maiman, CEO of IPG Health.[9] Public opinion confirms that sentiment: across seven countries, Edelman found that seven out of ten employees (69 percent) say societal impact is a strong expectation when considering a job, including working for a business that reflects their values.[10]

It is important to recognize that in an organization of any size, shared corporate values inevitably bump up against personal values.

A value such as respect may be easy to embrace in the abstract, but it becomes trickier when a leader's stance runs the risk of demoralizing employees who hold an opposing view.[11] Acknowledging that not everyone will agree can help create a culture in which colleagues become comfortable sharing opposing viewpoints with each other and at the same time enable leaders to stake out positions on issues that demand a response.[12] "I try to stress above all that we need to try to respect each other and treat each other with a sense of decency," said Dr. Paul Y. Song, CEO of NKGen Biotech.[13]

Many of the issues that CEOs have addressed in the past decade dealt with increasing diversity and inclusion or expanding human rights or civil rights. "The first value we focus on is that we want to be an inclusive workplace," said Arvind Krishna, CEO of IBM, who cited instances of the firm's practices dating back to the 1930s.[14] "So when it comes to issues like bathroom bills in North Carolina or transgender laws in Texas, we're willing to speak up and really get very vocal with state government." This underscores the importance of protecting and defending employees, particularly those in marginalized groups targeted by legislation that seeks to deny or restrict their rights.

Consistency: Committing to Core Beliefs

After the 2018 mass shooting at Marjory Stoneman Douglas High School in Parkland, Florida, Ed Stack, then CEO of Dick's Sporting Goods, decided that the chain would stop selling assault rifles and high-capacity magazines, and would require all gun buyers to be twenty-one years old or older. He did it for one reason: "If we do all those things and we save one life, in my mind it's all worth it."[15] It was a powerful statement from the heart that needed no explanation.

Firms seeking to appeal to the broadest possible customer base face a tension between being true to their values and paying a price for doing so. Customers say they have a clear preference: more than six out of ten (63 percent) in fourteen countries claim to buy or advocate for brands based on their beliefs and values.[16] Given the partisan divide in the United States, this can be a blessing or a curse. Ed Stack experienced this firsthand when his company's new firearms policy contributed to a decline in sales in the subsequent quarter.[17]

At the same time, the strength of a brand such as Patagonia with both liberals and conservatives suggests that if customers love a firm's

Values can make the case for "why."

products, they may admire (or at least forgive) the brand's consistency even if they don't share its views on specific issues.[18] Patagonia's move to pull its products out of Jackson Hole Mountain Resort after the resort hosted a fundraiser for members of Congress who denied the results of the 2020 presidential election put the company's values before the bottom line.[19] This stance is unquestionably easier when managers don't have to answer to investors.

Adaptability: Being Open to Growth

Learning is critical to more than technical innovation. The importance of understanding other people plays a significant role in performance and morale. Google's Project Aristotle crunched the numbers to determine the characteristics of its most effective teams, and it found that "success is often built on experiences—like emotional interactions and complicated conversations and discussions of who we want to be and how our teammates make us feel."[20]

After the murder of George Floyd, many business leaders sought to be frank about the reality that they were learning about systemic racism and the challenges faced by Black Americans. "Each of us, starting with me, must look at where we are as individuals, confront our fixed mindset and act," wrote Microsoft CEO Satya Nadella.[21] Nadella was not alone in expressing these sentiments at the time, but he did so in a manner that was both humble and matter-of-fact.

Particularly in moments of deep uncertainty, the willingness of leaders to admit that they don't know everything can boost their credibility. "I think there is tremendous opportunity for CEOs to stand in front of their team and say, 'I don't know what's happening. I don't know how this is going to end,'" said Jake Wood, founder and CEO of Groundswell.[22]

Mission: Cultivating a Sense of Purpose

The emergence of benefit corporations (or B Corps), purpose-driven capitalism, and other related trends speaks to the desire of many employees to engage in work that makes a positive contribution to society.[23] "Part of what's driving employees is they see, 'We're going to spend 60 hours a week, most of our productive working hours, trying to help this company, and we don't want to check our values and priorities at the time clock. We want the companies we work for to represent things that are important to us,'" said Alex Laskey, cofounder and former president of Opower, a company that helps consumers reduce their home energy usage.[24] When a company's line of business intersects with the political arena, whether the issue is climate change, health care, or immigration, the ability to connect to its employees' commitment to the mission can reinforce the importance of their efforts.

Mission: Aligning with the Strategic Direction

In some clear-cut cases, a values-based appeal can directly support a company's core business. When Nihar Malaviya, CEO of Penguin Random House, spoke out against book bans in Escambia County, Florida, he cited the capacity of books "to change lives for the better" and called the bans "a direct threat to democracy and our Constitutional rights."[25] But values can be more than a sorting mechanism that helps executives narrow their focus when deciding whether to address an issue. They can also serve the opposite function when a firm wants to increase its impact. "We think about our values, and we think about using any platform that we might have to expand those values," said Tim Cook of Apple, explaining how the company seeks to act on its commitment to the environment by "greening" its supply chain.[26] "We touch a lot of companies around the world because we manufacture things, and we know that we have a responsibility to convince those companies to use renewable energy, and to recycle, and to do things that are sustainable."

Restating the mission can also help to reorient a conversation. When asked how she planned to respond to twenty-one state attorneys general who warned her company about the retail sale of the abortion medication mifepristone in their states, CVS CEO Karen Lynch pivoted to values. "What is our North Star? Improve access, quality, and health for Americans. And we have been a strong proponent for many years in women's health," she said before answering that the company would "dispense drugs that are FDA-approved where legally permissible."[27] This enabled her an opportunity to connect with an important audience she wanted to reach without crossing a line or saying anything that would put the company in jeopardy.

Larry Fink framed his 2020 letter to CEOs as an outgrowth of the company's responsibility to its clients. That framing got buried in the political aftermath, but the statement was based on a values appeal of protecting customers' long-term interests. And as Fink and BlackRock found in the coming months and years, stakeholders who cared deeply about the impacts of climate change wanted the company to walk the walk.

Key Insights: Speaking from Values

Values can help to clarify a simple question—"What do we stand for?" —when an issue offers no easy answers.

1. *Use values as a filter.* If an issue doesn't have a clear connection to the firm's core business or values, it probably doesn't merit the chief executive's attention. "You can't comment on every single thing, otherwise it's just noise," said Arvind Krishna of IBM. "So you go back to your values."[28] An explanation based on values doesn't have to be complicated. Is it the right thing to do because of a core value or belief? If so, just come out and say it.

2. *Look for the intersection of values, culture, and employees.* Employees perform at their best when driven by a sense of meaning and purpose. "Anything you say has to be based in an appreciation and understanding of the values your company stands for," said Richard Socarides, former chief communications officer at GLG. "Each company has to evaluate every issue based on their values and what they stand for and what's important to their employees."[29]

3. *Focus on values to expand impact.* Values should inform every strategic decision a firm makes. This can include efforts to effect change among employees (e.g., committing to internal DEI initiatives), suppliers (e.g., improving practices across the supply chain), or customers (e.g., encouraging the reuse or recycling of company packaging or products). Values can make the case for why something matters.

9

VALUES ARE NOT ENOUGH

"It's not about saying anything fancy. You have to get things done."[1]

When he said this, former CEO of the Nature Conservancy Mark Tercek was referring to companies meeting the expectations of customers, shareholders, and suppliers on climate change, but his advice rings true regardless of the issue.

The say-do gap on climate change offers a telling example of the accountability challenge that corporations face. Most large global companies that have announced emissions targets for 2050 haven't yet addressed the critical part of the equation. "Sixty-three percent of the Fortune Global 500 have 2050 emissions targets . . . and nearly half have set more ambitious 2030 targets," said Paul Polman, former CEO of Unilever.[2] "But only around a third have set targets for so-called 'Scope 3' emissions, which come from their suppliers or the use of their products, despite the fact that Scope 3 emissions account for about 80% of the companies' total carbon footprint."

Climate is not the only issue on which rhetoric fails to match reality. More broadly, two-thirds of Americans (68 percent) believe corporate messaging about social issues is "a marketing ploy rather than an authentic opinion," according to an Axios Harris poll.[3] The Wells Fargo case and the studies by McKinsey and The Plug mentioned in chapter 5 offer a few examples of the walk not matching the talk on diversity initiatives and racial justice pledges.

Pinterest provides a cautionary tale of what can happen when a firm's external messaging doesn't match the internal reality. A few weeks after the murder of George Floyd, two Black women who had recently quit called the company out for promoting a public image that directly contradicted their experience there.[4] "As a Black woman, seeing @Pinterest's middle of the night 'Black employees matter' statement made me scratch my head after I just fought for over a full year to be paid and leveled fairly," tweeted former employee Ifeoma Ozoma.[5]

The public perceives these disconnects: Edelman found that six out of ten (62 percent), including majorities across all demographic groups, "believe companies are doing mediocre or worse living up to their promises and commitments to address racism both within their organization as well as the population."[6]

Accountability Check

In an era in which stakeholders are increasingly savvy about spin and greenwashing, an accountability check for any kind of public position should be a standard part of brand hygiene. The easiest way to practice this is to be clear in advance about the actions that will back the company's words.

"One of the guiding principles now with our leadership statements is making sure we're not seen as performative. That's always a tricky balance when we're talking about how a leader is using their platform to talk about a social issue. You don't want to make it look like they don't back it up with their actions," said Michelle Rodriguez of LinkedIn.[7] Before deciding to make an external statement, LinkedIn now considers if it will engage in continual learning on a topic, provide funding for an external organization, or make internal changes to address the issue. "If it's just to say something, we most likely won't do it," she said.

LinkedIn's approach doesn't make its decisions easier, but its clarity about the necessity of action can help it determine when *not* to take a position. These decisions are not just about public relations; they are critical to maintaining credibility with employees. While the downside of failing to back words with action is easy to imagine, companies that get it right also see a big potential upside. A Gartner study of five thousand employees found that organizational action on issues can lead to a significant increase in the percentage of highly engaged employees.[8]

Connect with values, and lead with actions.

Connect, Then Lead? Bottom Line Up Front?

The basic two-step between values and action can be summed up as *connect, then lead*: connect with values, and lead with actions.[9] The reasoning behind this is rooted in how our brains work. Emotion leads, logic follows. We respond first at a gut level, and then we look to analysis to support our intuition. A clear, concise action statement authenticates a values-based appeal as genuine.

PayPal CEO Dan Schulman used this model in his succinct response to North Carolina's 2016 law that restricted transgender peoples' use of public restrooms. He said, "The new law perpetuates discrimination and it violates the values and principles that are at the core of PayPal's mission and culture. As a result, PayPal will not move forward with our planned expansion into Charlotte."[10]

There are exceptions to this tried-and-true formula. It can be useful to state the action first when it has a material effect on a firm's core business. This was how BP structured its response to Russia's invasion of Ukraine: "The bp board today announced that bp will exit its shareholding in Rosneft."[11] After spelling out the headline business decision, the board chair and CEO offered personal statements that explained the rationale in terms of both the long-term shareholders' interest and "the right thing to do." In cases such as this, putting the action first provides clarity for markets, investors, and the media.

And it can be powerful to put the bottom line up front in a personal statement, as Ken Frazier did in announcing his departure from President Trump's business council after a white supremacist rally in Charlottesville, Virginia, in 2017. "I am resigning from the President's American Manufacturing Council," he wrote before explaining how values drove his decision. "America's leaders must honor our fundamental values by clearly rejecting expressions of hatred, bigotry, and group supremacy, which run counter to the American ideal that all people are created equal."[12] While speaking as the CEO of Merck, Frazier's personal perspective as a Black man lent implicit significance to his remarks.

Accountability through Networks and Disclosures

One way that companies can commit to accountability measures without having to start from scratch on every issue is by taking part in
networks that develop benchmarks and goals for corporate action. One
of the oldest and most established of these is Ceres. Founded in the
wake of the *Exxon Valdez* oil spill in 1989, Ceres began as a group of
investors that embraced environmental stewardship as a responsibility of the business community.[13] As climate change emerged as the
defining sustainability issue of the era, Ceres grew into a network of
more than 220 institutional investors with over $60 trillion in assets
under management as well as a network of dozens of the world's largest corporations in sectors ranging from banking to energy to food
and beverage.[14] Its members commit to targeted actions and benefit
from shared research and best practices that help them achieve their
sustainability goals.

In 2017 Ceres was one of five investor networks that came together
to cofound Climate Action 100+ in the wake of the 2015 Paris Agreement.[15] The investor-led initiative was formed to ensure that the largest corporate greenhouse gas emitters would take action on climate
change that is in line or consistent with the goal of the accord. Climate
Action 100+ was followed by the launching of the United Nations–led
Race to Zero campaign, the Net Zero Asset Managers initiative, and the
Glasgow Financial Alliance for Net Zero (GFANZ).

Such initiatives have come under heavy fire as part of the anti-ESG
backlash. As noted in chapter 4, Climate Action 100+ and GFANZ
drew the ire of nineteen Republican attorneys general who signed a
letter that accused BlackRock of putting the interests of these groups
ahead of its duty as a fiduciary for their states' pension funds.[16] Even before Republicans formally regained control of the US House of Representatives after the 2022 midterm elections, Rep. Jim Jordan (R-Ohio),
incoming chair of the House Judiciary Committee, announced an antitrust investigation of Climate Action 100+.[17] Other skeptics raised
questions about whether the expectations of these groups are achiev-
able, while some climate advocates dismissed them as efforts to maintain the corporate status quo.[18]

But networks can serve a broader purpose for corporations and executives trying to determine how to move forward on an issue. Respected organizations such as Ceres provide credible research that can help firms make informed decisions about action-oriented goals that are meaningful and realistic. Networks enforce accountability for commitments and require members to disclose information. This provides an easy way for stakeholders to track participants' progress, which can boost credibility.[19] Collective action also brings less visibility and less risk, which can work well if a firm wants to be a part of the pack rather than the leader of it.[20]

Climate change is not the only issue that has spawned networks of this sort. The CEO Action for Diversity & Inclusion initiative has solicited specific action commitments from hundreds of corporations in its network.[21] While this approach doesn't necessarily incentivize firms to push toward ambitious goals, it does offer clarity about what stakeholders can expect from them.

At the other end of the spectrum in terms of ambition, the Long-Term Stock Exchange (LTSE) is a securities exchange for companies that demonstrate a commitment to sustainable and equitable growth over the long term. Members of the LTSE are expected to address their environmental impact, diversity and inclusion efforts, community engagement, and investment in employees.[22] Similarly, the benefit corporation (B Corp) movement, while not a network, uses a certification system to verify that companies meet environmental, social, and governance standards that it has established through a global advisory council.[23] These types of initiatives can confer legitimacy if they operate transparently, hold members accountable for results, and achieve enough scale to offer companies a recognizable seal of approval for their efforts.

Even without networks, companies can make accountability part of their brand through voluntary disclosures.[24] Reports that document progress on diversity and inclusion, sustainability, and/or overall ESG performance are increasingly the norm for the world's largest corporations. Beyond these summaries, which often function as de facto appendixes of annual reports, corporations can share more standardized information such as EEO-1 filings, which are mandatory reports on workforce diversity that companies with more than a hundred employees must submit annually to the U.S. Equal Employment Opportunity Commission. As of August 2021, more than three-quarters of S&P 100 corporations disclosed their EEO-1 reports.[25] Racial justice audits driven by shareholder proposals have become more common after the murder of George Floyd, and corporations from Amazon to Citi have committed to conducting them.[26] The use of widely adopted standards, such as those developed and maintained by the Sustainability Accounting Standards Board or the Global Reporting Initiative, can help make the information companies share easier for stakeholders to evaluate.

The increasing pressure for transparency and disclosure presents an opportunity. Firms that offer consistent, reliable information year after year can tell a proactive story of successes and challenges over time and eliminate concerns about talking a lot and saying nothing.

Key Insights: Backing Values with Actions

Business leaders should expect employees, customers, and other key stakeholders to hold them accountable for bold words that are not supported by actions.

1. *Match the outside story with the inside story.* As the Pinterest case illustrates, a disconnect between external statements and internal behaviors runs the risk of turning off customers and demoralizing employees. In the worst-case scenario, it sets the table for a PR crisis when the story gets out, which it always does. "When people make commitments, look at how they treat their employees and their customers," said Eleanor Lacey, general counsel of Asana.[27]

2. *Connect values to action with a "that's why" statement.* Just as Aesop's fables end with a moral ("That's why slow and steady wins the race"), the story a company or its leader tells about its values should link clearly to its actions. Is the action internal or external? What is its intended impact? A compelling rationale for the course of action helps to minimize the possibility that a good-faith effort will be dismissed as a public relations stunt.

3. *Use accountability and transparency as a means of establishing credibility and trust.* Whether through voluntary disclosures or

participation in networks that set benchmarks on a single issue, the ultimate goal of these efforts from a communication standpoint is to build credibility and trust with stakeholders. This is not limited to political and social issues. A review of annual reports over a couple decades found that companies that explained failures in terms of "internal, controllable factors" had higher stock prices a year later than those that "pointed to external and uncontrollable factors."[28]

10

HAVE A PROCESS

There's an old joke among Washington insiders that the most dangerous place in the city is the ten feet between a senator and a TV camera. Speaking off the cuff about the issues of the day while basking in the glow of the spotlight is a time-honored tradition in the nation's capital. For the unprepared, it is also a recipe for unforced errors.

Though many business leaders tend in the opposite direction, social media has lowered the guardrails, making it effortless to fire off a tweet or LinkedIn post on the spur of the moment. Salesforce CEO Marc Benioff recalled that at the end of an evening after a few drinks, he tweeted his response to the passage of Indiana's Religious Freedom Restoration Act only to wake up the next day to discover that his tweet had blown up and reshaped the terms of the debate.[1] In Benioff's case, this worked out. Others shouldn't count on being so lucky. Mark Zuckerberg found this out when he waded into speculating about the intent of Holocaust deniers who post their views on Facebook.[2]

With issues emerging on a constant basis, it's important to have a decision-making process that can guide informed choices about if, when, and how to speak out. Every company has its own approach based on the complexity of the organization, the division of roles and responsibilities, and a handful of other factors, but the fundamental considerations are universal.

Relevance

The hardest question is often the first one: is the issue relevant? A handful of follow-up questions that have surfaced throughout the book can help to clarify questions of scope:

- How does the issue affect your core business?
- How does it relate to your mission?
- How does it relate to your stakeholders:
  - Employees?
  - Customers?
  - Board?
  - Investors/shareholders?
  - Suppliers?
- What's the right thing to do?

The last question is neither aspirational nor idealistic. Values matter the most. Many of the decisions that CEOs faced in the past decade about speaking out concerned the protection or expansion of the civil or human rights of their employees. More recently, as noted in chapter 5, divestment from Russia was not strictly a question of political risk management. There is always a moral dimension in play.

Game Plan

If an issue is within scope, stakeholder outreach precedes decisions about whether to speak out and what to say. When employees are the primary stakeholders, a healthy dialogue should inform whether the issue merits an internal or external response (see chapter 6, "Listen First"). An internal response is not inherently less risky—every internal communication should be expected to leak—but a message that not only addresses specific concerns and interests but also links clearly to action can help employees feel heard while reserving external channels for issues that either reach a threshold of urgency or importance or involve more stakeholders.

At the other end of the spectrum, anything with clear geopolitical or bottom-line implications starts at the board level and moves outward from there. For other issues that call for an external response, there are some questions to sort through at the strategic level:

- Are other companies speaking out on the issue? If so, is a joint statement an option to achieve the best outcome?

- What are the risks in speaking out? (See the section on "Risks" below.)
- What are the risks in saying nothing?
- What needs to be said?
  - Does it connect to the mission, people, or values?
  - Is there a clear plan to back words with action?
- If there will be a speaker, who is the best messenger for the issue?

More tactical considerations about where, when, and how to address an issue are critical and depend on an understanding of the context. Due diligence is a given, particularly when considering a collective action such as a letter or an amicus brief. Many of these efforts are organized by reputable third parties, but it's not always clear who is the organizing force behind the scenes and what their agenda is. This is where connections make the difference. Contacts in trade associations and advocacy organizations traffic in this information for a living, but personal networks are often the best sources for the inside story on the who, what, and why.

Stakeholder Math

A general best practice for improving the quality of decisions is finding creative ways to quantify decisions that seem fundamentally qualitative. It's no different than doing brand or message testing rather than following a hunch about whether a new idea will resonate with customers. Where taking a stance is concerned, this comes down to stakeholder math.

Professor Scott Galloway of New York University's Stern School of Business offered Nike's decision to feature former NFL quarterback Colin Kaepernick in an ad campaign as an example of how to run the numbers and arrive at an informed decision.[3] Kaepernick's football career ended after the 2016–17 season, during which he kneeled or refused to stand during the national anthem in protest of racial oppression in the United States.[4] After declaring himself a free agent at the end of that season, Kaepernick received no offers to play for other teams the following year. In the fall of 2018, Nike decided to make Kaepernick one of the faces of its thirtieth-anniversary celebration of its "Just Do It" campaign.[5]

At first glance, this appeared to be a risky move by Nike. Americans buy sneakers in both red states and blue ones, and a polarizing figure like Kaepernick might alienate half of those customers in a sharply divided country.

But the stakeholder math told a different story. "Two-thirds of Nike's business actually comes from outside of the United States," Galloway noted.[6] He pointed out that of the remaining third of its business in the United States, most buyers are younger than the age of thirty, and a significant share of those customers are people of color. Galloway continued,

> Some people are going to like this decision and see it as leadership and endorse it and feel good about it, and other people it's going to upset and they're going to think less of the Nike brand. But when you talk about the latter, when you take the two-thirds out of international, when you take the consumer base that is the US, you're really mathematically talking about, probably talking about 3–5% of Nike's revenue base is in the blast zone where they will think less of the brand.

Subsequent data supported this back-of-the-envelope calculation. Nike's stock initially dipped when the news of the ad broke, but six months later, the company had widened its lead over rival Adidas on the measure of customers' intent to purchase the brand.[7] Over the next four years, Nike's stock outperformed both its rival Adidas and the S&P 500. The Kaepernick ad is just one of many factors that affected the long-term trend in the stock price, but it certainly didn't tank the brand. A campaign that may have looked like a big risk on the surface turned out to be a much smaller one when viewed at a granular level.

Customer segmentation of this sort is the backbone of marketing analysis. The same techniques that help companies determine how a product might play in Peoria can be used to anticipate how a stance will be received. Where speaking out is concerned, research shows that a key variable is the degree of polarization among the target audience. An experiment found that when stakeholder opinions are fairly evenly divided (which researchers call symmetrical polarization), the average response to a stance is negative, but when opinions veer in one direction (asymmetrical polarization), there can be an upside to expressing a view that speaks to the majority.[8]

It's no surprise that preaching to the choir can stir the congregation, but the same research also yielded an unexpected result: in a highly polarized environment, companies can potentially expand their reach by playing against type.[9] The real-life case study that supports this finding has been dubbed the "Goya effect," a reference to the Hispanic-owned food company whose CEO made headlines in the summer of 2020 for praising Donald Trump. Goya's Latino customer base in the United States, which tends to lean Democratic, did not abandon the brand afterward, but Goya sales increased significantly in strongly Republican counties, evidence of a so-called buycott.[10] This doesn't mean that companies should cynically adopt contrarian positions for the sake of expanding their market share, but it provides a way to think about the math when a leader is considering a stance that breaks with expectations.

Risks: What If?

While it is not possible to predict stakeholder reactions with certainty, there are ways to analyze the potential risks involved with taking a high-stakes stance. Some involve typical tools of the trade in corporate communications, while others are borrowed from contexts that focus on decision-making.

The anti-ESG backlash from governors and attorneys general provides a playbook for anticipating partisan responses to positions on environmental and social issues. Recent history has shown that retaliation and retribution are the price for failing loyalty tests (Delta, Disney) or for changing business practices that affect industries with powerful political backers such as fossil fuel companies (BlackRock) or firearms manufacturers (Citi, JPMorgan). On the other side of the spectrum, leaders in New York City and California have made clear that they expect corporations to address their constituents' preferences on issues ranging from climate change (financial services and big banks) to access to reproductive health care (Walgreens).

Gut feel should be tempered by ground truth.

For anything involving media interviews, preparing an "attacks and responses" road map should be standard operating procedure. This simple document has two columns consisting of difficult questions on the left ("When They Ask") and well-crafted answers on the right ("You Say"). The goal is to work through the dozen or so most challenging, devious, or otherwise dreaded questions that might come up, minimizing the risks of "live thinking" when pressed on a tricky subject.

Given the partisan divisions in the United States and the inherently political nature of some issues that business leaders confront, scenario planning, murder boards, or red teaming can be useful for thinking through possible what-ifs. This doesn't require the rigor of the Naval War College to prove valuable. Assign team members to represent the views of investors, board members, customers, politicians, regulators, advocates, journalists, and so on, and run the game. This exercise can help uncover blind spots, identify hot buttons that might escalate tensions, and sharpen thinking about likelihoods and consequences. On a smaller scale, appointing a devil's advocate to probe weaknesses from every conceivable angle can serve a similar purpose. (*Note:* The most effective devil's advocates are the ones who can express authentic dissent rather than just voicing the arguments of the other side.[11])

To promote this kind of thinking, social psychologist Gary Klein came up with a novel tool that he called a premortem.[12] Klein devised it to examine consequential project management decisions, and it is easy to envision its utility in this context. All it requires is a meeting of the key participants in the decision-making process. The attendees each write up their own answers to a hypothetical question: *Imagine it is a year after the decision was made. It was a disaster. What happened?*

Unlike a brainstorming or red team meeting, a premortem benefits from individual contributions that are not tainted by social contagion effects such as the loudest voices in the room drowning out or silencing the rest. It empowers pessimists to think creatively about worst-case scenarios without fear of being chastised for voicing unpopular views. The ultimate decision-makers can simply use the results to surface overlooked or unimagined possibilities. Premortem analysis has become an accepted practice in some corners of the Department of Defense and in a wide range of other organizations.

Some of these techniques may sound like overkill. But given the complexity of making decisions with global implications, such as BP's exiting its Rosneft partnership after Russia's invasion of Ukraine, there is good reason to take as much care as possible when figuring out what to say and how to say it.

Key Insights: Making Better Decisions

To paraphrase Warren Buffett, a reputation built over years can be destroyed in a matter of minutes. Process offers no guarantees, but it builds in the opportunity to think carefully before speaking.

1. *Include quality control in the decision-making process.* Decisions about speaking out can have good or bad outcomes for a variety of reasons. The quality of the decision-making process shouldn't be one of them. An effective process can be light or rigorous depending on the size of the organization and the circumstances, but the probability of an unforced error goes up if people are checking their own homework.
2. *Pressure test ideas.* The graveyard of failed messaging and branding campaigns is filled with ideas that sounded good to the people in the room at the time. Actively solicit adversarial opinions that probe, point to weaknesses, and unmask hidden liabilities. As the saying goes, feedback is a gift.
3. *Quantify the qualitative.* Whether the key stakeholders are employees or customers, gut feel should be tempered by ground truth. In the absence of complete data, even rough numbers can yield valuable insights that lead to better decisions about if, when, and how to take a stance.
4. *Recognize the inconsistencies.* Given the competing interests that any business has to juggle, some decisions will be more imperfect than others. A multinational that stakes out a position as a defender of human rights in one country will inevitably find itself

between a rock and a hard place in another where strategic necessity leads to a degree of compromise. Being clear-eyed about these trade-offs goes with the territory.

5. *Don't lose sight of the basics.* "What you need to do is tell the truth," said Mark Tercek, former CEO of the Nature Conservancy. "Have a simple plan and tell the truth."[13]

AFTERWORD

From racial justice to divestment from Russia, corporations and their leaders have had to navigate significant political and social currents in recent years. Depending on the issue and the industry, some have tried to ride the waves, while others have resisted the tide.

At the turn of the twenty-first century, Ian H. Wilson, a longtime veteran of General Electric's strategic planning team, proposed a model to describe how corporations respond to changes in the sociopolitical environment. "As new societal wants, needs, and expectations develop, corporations tend to progress through a series of seven stages of reaction, from initial outright rejection to ultimate strategic assimilation," he wrote.[1] Using language that echoed Elisabeth Kübler-Ross's stages of grief, he offered the following progression:

- Dismissal
- Outrage
- Counterattack
- Experimentation
- Compliance
- "The PR Phase"
- Strategic Assimilation

This model describes some of the dynamics that have come up in this book. Corporate responses to calls for action on climate change, for instance, can be found at nearly every point along Wilson's continuum, from the angry counterattacks by political allies of fossil fuel companies to PR efforts such as Walmart's "Project Gigaton" to the strategic assimilation of Apple as it pushes sustainability measures down its supply chain.

As stakeholders have begun demanding more from corporations than in the past, some business leaders have pushed back. Others have engaged in new ways and experimented openly in the public sphere.

Howard Schultz's 2013 letter to customers asking them to leave their guns at home, Marc Benioff's tweets that helped push for changes in Indiana's Religious Freedom Restoration Act in 2015, the collective response of CEOs who opposed North Carolina's House bill 2 in 2016, and Larry Fink's 2020 letter to CEOs—all were outside the realm of imagination at the turn of the century. Experimentation inherently leads to both successes and failures that inform future decisions.

On matters of workforce diversity, equity, and inclusion, many large corporations have moved into a phase that could be described as compliance (e.g., disclosures and racial equity audits), while those on the leading edge seem poised for strategic assimilation. The catch, of course, is that progress is neither uniform nor linear. An annual analysis of trends in the membership composition of Fortune 500 companies' boards found that between 2021 and 2022, the share of board director seats going to women decreased by five percentage points (45 percent in 2021 to 40 percent in 2022), and the share of seats going to racial or ethnic minorities decreased by seven points (41 percent to 34 percent). Most noticeably, the percentage of seats going to Black directors dropped nine percentage points (26 percent to 19 percent), after a two-year spike precipitated by heightened awareness in 2020 of glaring disparities in racial equity.[2] The Supreme Court decision in June 2023 that undid affirmative action for college admissions may have far-reaching effects on corporate diversity initiatives. At this point, the only clear thing is that politicians who oppose DEI are poised for battle on this front. At the same time, DEI advocates will continue to use all the tools at their disposal to pressure corporations to achieve more ambitious benchmarks and will hold them accountable when they fail to do so.

Wilson characterized "the PR phase" as a recognition that adopting new rules could bring public relations rewards.[3] Communications such as the Business Roundtable's 2019 "Statement on the Purpose of a Corporation" fit that description, as do the high-profile pledges that came in the wake of the murder of George Floyd. Wilson offered a note of caution about PR efforts ("any image must be clearly grounded in reality, if it is to last"), emphasizing the importance of achieving results that could stand up to objective measures.

Opponents of CEOs using their voices to engage on pressing political issues are unlikely to commit to a broader agenda of reducing corporate influence in politics. Under the prevailing status quo, they have little incentive to do so; the lobbying industrial complex is safely entrenched. Those who raise concerns about the legitimacy of CEOs' speaking out can enhance their own credibility by focusing on the forest rather than the trees.

Two Paths Forward

As issues emerge that demand the attention of corporate leaders, it may be helpful to think about two paths for reaching primary stakeholders. They are by no means mutually exclusive—today's internal statement is tomorrow's leak—but there are different thresholds and dynamics that drive and shape external and internal communication.

External Communication

As global pressure for transparent, standardized corporate reporting increases on issues such as risks stemming from climate change,[4] it is possible to imagine the communication becoming more routine and less exceptional. At the same time, political partisanship in the United States shows no sign of diminishing. As long as politicians have an incentive to fan the flames of the culture wars by acting to restrict civil and human rights, business leaders will have a responsibility to protect their employees. And when politicians threaten American democratic institutions that underpin the free enterprise system, corporate leaders will be pressed to fill the void. Multinationals doing business in countries that restrict or violate human rights as a matter of policy will always face complex challenges that require creative solutions where possible and clarity about the impact of imperfect compromises.

More broadly, the push and pull between shareholders and stakeholders will continue. While experts in corporate governance debate if stakeholder capitalism can survive in a system designed to benefit shareholders,[5] chief executives should maintain bilingual fluency in these conversations. When advocating for employees, customers, suppliers, or communities, or when taking positions on geopolitical developments, CEOs should be prepared to make their cases in terms of long-term value creation or risk management.

Internal Communication

Where employees are concerned, it is hard to imagine the balance swinging to a new normal in which sociopolitical issues disappear entirely from the office. As of this writing, during a season of layoffs in 2023, the balance of power between employers and employees has moved in the direction of employers on issues such as working remotely versus in the office,[6] but there is no indication at this point that this shift has led to a silencing of employees. Gen Zers and millennials have different views than older workers about the importance of addressing political and social issues,[7] and as they come to dominate the workforce, they will exert greater influence on everything from workplace norms to broader questions of how businesses should engage on the most pressing concerns affecting their employees, customers, suppliers, and investors.

If the changes since the beginning of the twenty-first century offer any indication of what's ahead, two things seem clear: radical uncertainty and demands for corporate action in the public interest are both here to stay. Private sector leaders should expect that the need to communicate about issues that are not business as usual will remain a vital part of their job.

ACKNOWLEDGMENTS

This book would not have been possible without the assistance, support, and wisdom of dozens of people.

Hilary Claggett, my editor at Georgetown University Press, believed in the possibility of this project from the start and was an invaluable sounding board every step of the way. Beth Weinberger's research assistance and common sense helped immensely with part I. John Neffinger and Larry Prusak provided invaluable gut checks and suggestions on various sections. Atta Tarki served as a tremendous source of perspective. Betsy Kohut's research assistance and infinite patience were essential from the first word to the last.

I am grateful to many friends and colleagues who generously shared their time, insights, and suggestions: Cameron Anderson, Ronit Avni, Julie Battilana, David Berkey, Vanessa Burbano, Matt Canter, Shana Carroll, Nicholas Cohn, Claudia Deane, Samantha Dodge, Sherrell Dorsey, David Ehrlich, George Elfond, Alison Byrne Fields, David Fischer, Michael Fischer, Sarah Fischer, Jeri Harman, Eben Harrell, Jenny He, Ed Hoffman, Caleb Keller, Eleanor Lacey, Alex Laskey, Jayme Link, Mindy Lubber, Dana Maiman, Noam Maital, Tanya Meck, Scott Metzger, Kevin O'Meara, Seth Pendleton, Tim Roberts, Michelle Rodriguez, Susann Roth, Sara Sciammacco, Richard Socarides, Dr. Paul Y. Song, Jeffrey Sonnenfeld, Jessica Spano, Sameer Srivastava, Greg Stone, Mark Tercek, Chido Tsemunhu, Jaime Vinck, and David Yermack.

All errors, shortcomings, and limitations are strictly my own.

NOTES

Preface

1. Ian Bremmer and Cliff Kupchan, *Top Risks 2022* (New York: Eurasia Group, 2022), 20, https://www.eurasiagroup.net/files/upload/EurasiaGroup_TopRisks2022.pdf.

2. Hambrick and Wowak, "CEO Sociopolitical Activism."

3. See Goodman, *Davos Man*; Giridharadas, *Winner Takes All*; Braden Wallake, "This Will Be the Most Vulnerable Thing I'll Ever Share," LinkedIn, August 9, 2022, https://www.linkedin.com/posts/bradenwallake_this-will-be-the-most-vulnerable-thing-ill-activity-6962886723617910784-_L4w/; and Karen Weise, "Social Media Was a C.E.O.'s Bullhorn, and How He Lured Women," *New York Times*, August 18, 2022, https://www.nytimes.com/2022/08/18/technology/dan-price-resign-social-media.html.

4. Rumstadt and Kanbach, "CEO Activism," 308.

5. Sonnenfeld, *Corporate Views*, 3.

6. Chatterji and Toffel, "New CEO Activists."

7. Fos, Kempf, and Tsoutsoura, "Political Polarization," 2.

8. Yevhen Tsymbalenko et al., "The Role of Company's Top Officials in Corporate Communications," *Problems and Perspectives in Management* 18, no. 3 (September 2020): 261, doi:10.21511/ppm.18(3).2020.22.

9. Wowak, Busenbark, and Hambrick, "How Do Employees React?," 554.

10. Julie Creswell and Matt Richtel, "Big Tobacco Heralds a Healthier World while Fighting Its Arrival," *New York Times*, November 6, 2022, updated November 7, 2022, https://www.nytimes.com/2022/11/06/health/tobacco-fda-menthol-ban-nicotine.html; and BP, "bp Parent Company Name Change Following AGM Approval," May 1, 2001, https://web.archive.org/web/20110806140152/http://www.bp.com/genericarticle.do?categoryId=2012968&contentId=2001578.

11. Brian Chesky, "Bonus Episode!," interview by Kara Swisher and Scott Galloway, at *Pivot* MIA, Vox Media, February 19, 2022, 25:18–25:23, https://en.padverb.com/er/pivot_nymag_rss-19-feb-2022-bonus-episode-live-from-pivot-mia-kara-scott-in-conversation-with-brian-chesky-ceo-of-airbnb.

12. Tsymbalenko et al., "Role of Company's Top Officials," 261.

13. Tsymbalenko et al., 262. See also Edelman, *Edelman Trust Barometer 2022: The Changing Role of the Corporation in Society* (Edelman Trust Institute with Harvard Business School, May 2022 update) 24, https://www.edelman.com/sites/g/files/aatuss191/files/2022-10/2022%20Edelman%20Trust%20Barometer%20Special%20Analysis%20Role%20of%20Business%20BIGs%20FINAL_10%2020PM

.pdf. This analysis finds significantly more support for using the CEO than the chief communications officer to respond to a contentious social or geopolitical issue.

14. John Neffinger and Matthew Kohut, *Compelling People: The Hidden Qualities That Make Us Influential* (New York: Plume, 2014), 216.

15. Andrew Jones, "How Companies Can Address the ESG Backlash," Conference Board, August 1, 2023,15, https://www.conference-board.org/pdfdownload .cfm?masterProductID=47725. See also Eleanor Hawkins, "America's CEOs Have Gone Silent on National Tragedies," *Axios*, February 2, 2023, https://www.axios.com /2023/02/02/americas-ceos-have-gone-silent-on-national-tragedies#.

16. Rumstadt and Kanbach, "CEO Activism," 307.

17. Stephen A. Greyser, "Johnson & Johnson: The Tylenol Tragedy," Harvard Business School Case 583-043, October 12, 1982 (revised May 1992), https://hbsp .harvard.edu/product/583043-PDF-ENG.

1. A New Part of the Job

1. Larry Fink, "Larry Fink's 2020 Letter to CEOs: A Fundamental Reshaping of Finance," BlackRock, 2020, https://www.blackrock.com/americas-offshore/en/lar ry-fink-ceo-letter. While Fink's letter was not dated, the *New York Times* reported it in January: Andrew Ross Sorkin, "New Lodestar for BlackRock: Climate Crisis," *New York Times*, January 14, 2020, https://www.nytimes.com/2020/01/14/business /dealbook/larry-fink-blackrock-climate-change.html.

2. Sorkin, "New Lodestar for BlackRock."

3. See, for instance, Hazel Bradford, "Climate Activists Say BlackRock Failing to Lead on Carbon Transition," *Pensions & Investments*, April 27, 2021, https://www.pi online.com/esg/climate-activists-say-blackrock-failing-lead-carbon-transition.

4. Letter from Giuseppe Bivona and Marco Taricco, Bluebell Capital Partners, to Larry Fink, November 10, 2022, https://static.foxbusiness.com/foxbusiness.com /content/uploads/2022/12/Bluebell-Partners-letter-to-BlackRock-10-November -2022.pdf. See also Evan Halper, "Is BlackRock's Larry Fink Blowing It for the Climate?," *Washington Post*, May 6, 2023, https://www.washingtonpost.com/busi ness/2023/05/06/blackrock-esg-climate-woke/.

5. Erin Arvedlund, "Vanguard Takes Institutional Lead over BlackRock," *Pensions & Investments*, June 12, 2023, https://www.pionline.com/largest-money-man agers/vanguard-pulls-ahead-blackrock-worldwide-institutional-assets; and Lananh Nguyen and Simon Jessop, "Davos 2023: BlackRock U.S. Inflows Dwarf $4 Bln Lost in ESG Backlash—CEO," Reuters, January 17, 2023, https://www.reuters.com /business/finance/davos-2023-blackrock-us-inflows-dwarf-4-bln-lost-esg-backlash -ceo-2023-01-17/.

6. BlackRock, *Annual Report 2010* (New York: BlackRock, 2010), 8, https://s24 .q4cdn.com/856567660/files/doc_financials/2010/ar/2010-Annual-Report.pdf.

7. Dana Canedy, "As the Main Character in 'Ellen' Comes Out, Some Companies See an Opportunity; Others Steer Clear," *New York Times*, April 30, 1997, https:// www.nytimes.com/1997/04/30/business/main-character-ellen-comes-some-com panies-see-opportunity-others-steer-clear.html.

8. Khadeeja Safdar, "Meet the New Nike Boss: Trading Tech for Air Jordans," *Wall Street Journal*, February 8, 2020, https://www.wsj.com/articles/meet-the-new-nike-boss-trading-tech-for-air-jordans-11581166802.

9. Monica Langley, "Salesforce's Marc Benioff Has Kicked Off New Era of Corporate Social Activism," *Wall Street Journal*, May 2, 2016, https://www.wsj.com/articles/salesforces-marc-benioff-has-kicked-off-new-era-of-corporate-social-activism-1462201172.

10. Howard Schultz, "Our Respectful Request," Starbucks Stories & News, September 17, 2013, https://stories.starbucks.com/press/2013/open-letter-from-howard/.

11. Myles Collier, "Chick-fil-A President Says 'God's Judgment' Coming Because of Same-Sex Marriage," *Christian Post*, July 18, 2012, https://www.christianpost.com/news/chick-fil-a-president-says-gods-judgment-coming-because-of-same-sex-marriage-78485/#SUuZKIUR05MhCW2p.99.

12. Peter Behr, "GE's Immelt Says U.S. Policy Deadlock Holds Back Clean Energy Development," *New York Times*, September 24, 2010, https://archive.nytimes.com/www.nytimes.com/cwire/2010/09/24/24climatewire-ges-immelt-says-us-policy-deadlock-holds-bac-86164.html.

13. John Mackey, "The Whole Foods Alternative to ObamaCare: Eight Things We Can Do to Improve Health Care without Adding to the Deficit," *Wall Street Journal*, August 11, 2009, https://www.wsj.com/articles/SB10001424052970204251404574342170072865070.

14. Megan Armstrong, Eathyn Edwards, and Duwain Pinder, "Corporate Commitments to Racial Justice: An Update," McKinsey Institute for Black Economic Mobility, February 21, 2023, 4, https://www.mckinsey.com/bem/our-insights/corporate-commitments-to-racial-justice-an-update.

15. Conference Board, "Survey: One in Ten Companies Publicly Responded to Supreme Court Ruling on Reproductive Rights," July 19, 2022, https://www.conference-board.org/press/supreme-court-ruling-on-reproductive-rights.

16. Andrew Ross Sorkin, "Michael Dell Is Trying to Be Nice," *New York Times*, October 9, 2021, https://www.nytimes.com/2021/10/09/business/dealbook/michael-dell-book.html.

17. Ramaswamy, *Woke, Inc.*, 18.

18. Mitch McConnell, "McConnell: Corporations Shouldn't Fall for Absurd Disinformation on Voting Laws," April 5, 2021, https://www.republicanleader.senate.gov/newsroom/press-releases/mcconnell-corporations-shouldnt-fall-for-absurd-disinformation-on-voting-laws.

19. Noel Randewich and Tiyashi Datta, "Apple's Market Value Ends above $3 Trillion for First Time," Reuters, June 30, 2023, https://www.reuters.com/technology/apples-market-value-breaches-3-trillion-mark-again-2023-06-30/.

20. Amanda Macias and Michael Sheetz, "Pentagon Awards SpaceX with Ukraine Contract for Starlink Satellite Internet," CNBC, June 1, 2023, https://www.cnbc.com/2023/06/01/pentagon-awards-spacex-with-ukraine-contract-for-starlink-satellite-internet.html.

21. National Shooting Sports Foundation, "NSSF Board of Governors," last

updated July 17, 2023, https://www.nssf.org/about-us/nssf-board-of-governors/; and
Everytown for Gun Safety, "The Gun Industry's Power Broker," Everytown Research
& Policy, January 12, 2023, 7, https://everytownresearch.org/report/the-gun-indus
trys-power-broker-nssf/.

22. Stephen Gandel, "The Texas Law That Has Banks Saying They Don't 'Discriminate' against Guns," *New York Times*, May 28, 2022, updated May 29, 2022,
https://www.nytimes.com/2022/05/28/business/dealbook/texas-banks-gun-law
.html.

23. Paul Griffin, *The Carbon Majors Database: CDP Carbon Majors Report 2017*
(London: CDP Worldwide, 2017), 14, http://climateaccountability.org/pdf/Carbon
MajorsRpt2017%20Jul17.pdf. I am grateful to Julie Battilana for bringing this to
my attention.

24. Jeffrey Sonnenfeld, "People Trust Executives to Intervene in Social Issues,
Says Jeffrey Sonnenfeld," *The Economist*, September 14, 2022, https://www.econom
ist.com/by-invitation/2022/09/14/people-trust-executives-to-intervene-in-social-is
sues-says-jeffrey-sonnenfeld.

25. Stavros Gadinis and Christopher Havasy, "The Quest for Legitimacy: A Public Law Blueprint for Corporate Governance," April 11, 2022, 36, http://dx.doi.org
/10.2139/ssrn.4081543.

26. Mintzberg, *Nature of Managerial Work*, 76.

27. Tsymbalenko et al., "Role of Company's Top Officials," 261.

28. Chatterji and Toffel, "New CEO Activists."

29. Edelman, *Edelman Trust Barometer 2022: Global Report* (Edelman, 2022), 29,
https://www.edelman.com/sites/g/files/aatuss191/files/2022-01/2022%20Edel
man%20Trust%20Barometer%20FINAL_Jan25.pdf.

30. Edelman, *Changing Role of the Corporation*, 22.

31. Jordan Marlatt, *What Consumers Expect from CEOs* (Morning Consult, November 2022), 6, https://go.morningconsult.com/rs/850-TAA-511/images/221027
_CEO-Report.pdf.

32. Jennifer Tonti, "JUST Capital's 2021 Americans' Views on Business Survey:
Survey Analysis," JUST Capital, 2021, https://justcapital.com/reports/survey-anal
ysis-americans-agree-ceos-have-a-role-to-play-in-addressing-income-inequality-beli
eve-workers-are-being-left-behind/. See also this 2018 finding that two-thirds (65
percent) believe CEOs of large companies should use their position and potential
influence to advocate on behalf of social, environmental, or political issues they care
about personally: David F. Larcker et al., "The Double-Edged Sword of CEO Activism," Rock Center for Corporate Governance at Stanford University Closer Look
Series: Topics, Issues and Controversies in Corporate Governance No. CGRP-74,
Stanford University Graduate School of Business Research Paper 19-5, November
8, 2018, 4, https://www.df.cl/noticias/site/docs/20181221/20181221172221/ceo_ac
tivismo.pdf.

33. Tonti, "2021 Americans' Views on Business Survey"; and Global Strategy
Group and SEC Newgate, "ESG Monitor: United States Report, 2022 Research
Findings," 2022, 3, https://globalstrategygroup.com/wp-content/uploads/2012/07
/SEC-Newgate-ESG-Monitor-2022_Final.pdf.

34. Raffaella Sadun et al., "The C-Suite Skills That Matter Most," *Harvard Business Review* 100, no. 7–8 (2022), https://hbr.org/2022/07/the-c-suite-skills-that-matter-most.

35. Andrew Ross Sorkin, "Howard Schultz: Starbucks Is Battling for the 'Hearts and Minds' of Workers," *New York Times*, June 11, 2022, https://www.nytimes.com/2022/06/11/business/dealbook/howard-schultz-starbucks.html.

36. Rumstadt and Kanbach, "CEO Activism," 318.

37. Chesky interview by Swisher and Galloway, 33:31–33:34.

38. Chris Isidore, "United CEO Says the Employer Mandate Is the Best Way to Raise Vaccination Rates," CNN Business, September 16, 2021, https://www.cnn.com/2021/09/16/business/united-ceo-vaccine-mandates/index.html.

39. Dana Maiman, in discussion with author, October 17, 2022.

40. Chip Bergh, interview by Gillian Tett, Aspen Ideas Festival, Colorado, June 26, 2023, 28:13–28:27, https://www.youtube.com/watch?v=gO-Cy_gyowg.

41. Hambrick and Wowak, "CEO Sociopolitical Activism," 39.

42. Austin Carr, "The Inside Story of Starbucks's Race Together Campaign, No Foam," *Fast Company*, June 15, 2015, https://www.fastcompany.com/3046890/the-inside-story-of-starbuckss-race-together-campaign-no-foam.

43. Charles Riley, "Salesforce CEO: We're Helping Employees Move out of Indiana," CNN Money, April 2, 2015, https://money.cnn.com/2015/04/01/news/salesforce-benioff-indiana-religious-freedom-law/index.html.

44. Weber Shandwick/KRC Research, "The Dawn of CEO Activism," June 21, 2016, 8, https://cms.webershandwick.com/wp-content/uploads/2023/01/the-dawn-of-ceo-activism-2.pdf.

45. Hambrick and Wowak, "CEO Sociopolitical Activism," 43–45.

46. Civic Alliance, "Joint Statement on Protecting Voting Access," April 2, 2021, https://www.civicalliance.com/votingaccess.

47. Hambrick and Wowak, "CEO Sociopolitical Activism," 45.

48. Karthik Venkataraman et al., "Making Business Do Better for Everyone," Bain & Company, June 27, 2023, https://www.bain.com/insights/making-business-do-better-for-everyone/.

49. Satya Nadella, "Bonus Episode: Satya Nadella at Code Conference 2021," interview by Kara Swisher and Scott Galloway, *Pivot*, Vox Media, October 13, 2021, 45:00–45:09, 46:49.

50. Richard Edelman (blog), "Why I Signed," Edelman, April 16, 2021, https://www.edelman.com/insights/why-i-signed.

51. GLG, "The GLG CEO Survey: 2023," January 2023, 19, https://assets.glginsights.com/wp-content/uploads/2023/01/GLG_CEOSurvey_Guide.pdf.

52. Pew Research Center, "As Partisan Hostility Grows, Signs of Frustration with the Two-Party System," August 9, 2022, https://www.pewresearch.org/politics/2022/08/09/as-partisan-hostility-grows-signs-of-frustration-with-the-two-party-system/.

53. David Gelles, "Whole Foods Founder: The Whole World Is Getting Fat," *New York Times*, September 24, 2020, https://www.nytimes.com/2020/09/24/business/john-mackey-corner-office-whole-foods.html.

54. Jaime Vinck, in discussion with the author, June 30, 2022.

55. Brian Armstrong, "Coinbase Is a Mission Focused Company," Coinbase (blog), September 27, 2020, https://blog.coinbase.com/coinbase-is-a-mission-fo cused-company-af882df8804.

56. O'Ryan Johnson, "'I'm Not Being a D*ck': Kaseya CEO Voccola's Freewheel-ing Town Hall Spotlights Culture Clash with Incoming Datto Employees," *CRN*, July 19, 2022, https://www.crn.com/news/managed-services/-i-m-not-being-a-d-ck -kaseya-ceo-voccola-s-freewheeling-town-hall-spotlights-culture-clash-with-incom ing-datto-employees.

57. Kara Swisher, "American Airlines C.E.O. on Why He's Not Requiring You, or His Workers, to Be Vaccinated" (transcript of Doug Parker, interview by Kara Swisher, *Sway*), *New York Times*, August 5, 2021, https://www.nytimes.com/2021 /08/05/opinion/sway-kara-swisher-doug-parker.html.

58. Maiman discussion with author.

59. Alina Tugend, "For C.E.O.s, Communication Has Become a High-Wire Act," *New York Times*, December 7, 2022, https://www.nytimes.com/2022/12/07/busi ness/dealbook/ceo-communication.html.

60. Jamie Dimon, "'Axios on HBO': Jamie Dimon on China, His Salary and Racial Equity," interview by Jim VandeHei, *Axios*, October 4, 2021, https://www .axios.com/2021/10/04/jamie-dimon-china-uyghurs.

61. Missouri attorney general Andrew Bailey, "Attorney General Bailey Directs Letter to CVS and Walgreens over Distribution of Abortion Pills," press release, February 1, 2023, https://ago.mo.gov/home/news/2023/02/01/attorney-general -bailey-directs-letter-to-cvs-and-walgreens-over-distribution-of-abortion-pills.

62. Kaitlyn Radde and Sarah McCammon, "Walgreens Won't Sell Abortion Pills in Red States That Threatened Legal Action," NPR, March 4, 2023, https://www .npr.org/2023/03/04/1161143595/walgreens-abortion-pill-mifepristone-republican -threat-legal-action.

63. Governor Gavin Newsom, "Governor Newsom: California Pulls Back Re-newal of Walgreens Contract," press release, March 8, 2023, https://www.gov.ca .gov/2023/03/08/governor-newsom-california-pulls-back-renewal-of-walgreens-con tract/.

64. Johnson, "'I'm Not Being a D*ck.'"

65. Marty Swant, "Silence Is Not an Option: Research Shows Consumers Expect CEOs to Take a Stand on Political Issues," *Forbes*, April 19, 2021, https://www.forb es.com/sites/martyswant/2021/04/19/silence-is-not-an-option-research-shows -consumers-expect-ceos-to-take-a-stand-on-political-issues/.

66. Stephanie Mehta, "'It Was Not an Issue I Wanted to Get Involved With': Del-ta's CEO on Voting Rights and More," *Fast Company*, May 26, 2021, https://www.fa stcompany.com/90639713/it-was-not-an-issue-i-wanted-to-get-involved-with-deltas -ceo-on-voting-rights-and-more.

67. Aidin Vaziri, "Spotify Loses $4 Billion in Market Value Following Neil Young Controversy," *San Francisco Chronicle*, January 28, 2022, https://datebook.sfchron icle.com/music/spotify-loses-4-billion-in-market-value-following-neil-young-con troversy.

68. Ashley Carman, "Spotify CEO Defends Joe Rogan Deal in Tense Company Town Hall / He Says Spotify Is a Platform for Rogan, but Publisher for Gimlet," *The Verge*, February 3, 2022, https://www.theverge.com/2022/2/3/22915456/spoti fy-ceo-joe-rogan-daniel-ek-town-hall-speech-platform-podcast.

69. *State of Washington et al. v. Donald J. Trump et al.*, No. 17-35105, Appendix A (9th Cir. 2017), https://cdn.ca9.uscourts.gov/datastore/general/2017/02/06/17-351 05%20amicus%20tech%20companies.pdf.

70. Petition created by Irene Scher, "To: Oracle Leadership, Petition for Oracle to Sign the Immigrant Amicus Brief," Coworker.org, 2017, https://www.coworker.org /petitions/petition-for-oracle-to-sign-the-immigrant-amicus-brief.

71. Swisher, "American Airlines C.E.O."

72. Bondi, Burbano, and Dell'Acqua, "When to Talk Politics," 33.

73. Rumstadt and Kanbach, "CEO Activism," 320.

74. Edelman, *Edelman Trust Barometer 2022 Special Report: Trust in the Workplace* (Edelman, 2022), 30, 5, https://www.edelman.com/sites/g/files/aatuss191/files/20 22-08/2022%20Edelman%20Trust%20Barometer%20Special%20Report%20 Trust%20in%20the%20Workplace%20FINAL.pdf.

75. Edelman, *2023 Edelman Trust Barometer Special Report: Business and Racial Justice* (Edelman, 2023), 13, https://www.edelman.com/sites/g/files/aatuss191/files /2023-05/2023%20Edelman%20Trust%20Barometer%20Special%20Report%20 Business%20and%20Racial%20Justice%20FINAL.pdf.

76. Edelman, 14.

77. Edelman, *Trust in the Workplace*, 15.

78. Edelman, 16.

79. Larcker et al., "Double-Edged Sword," 4.

80. Wowak, Busenbark, and Hambrick, "How Do Employees React?," 581.

81. Burbano, "Demotivating Effects."

82. Rumstadt and Kanbach, "CEO Activism," 320.

83. See, for instance, Keshab Acharya, Michael A. Abebe, and Mark Kroll, "The Influence of CEO Political Outspokenness on Stock Market Reaction and Firm Performance," *Academy of Management Proceedings* 2019, no. 1 (August 2019): 13959, https://doi.org/10.5465/AMBPP.2019.25; and Anahit Mkrtchyan, Jason Sandvik, and Vivi Zhu, "CEO Activism and Firm Value," March 2022, http://dx.doi.org/10 .2139/ssrn.3699082.

84. Michael T. Durney et al., "CEO (In)Activism and Investor Decisions," June 30, 2020, http://dx.doi.org/10.2139/ssrn.3604321.

85. Global Strategy Group, "The Shifting Politics of Doing Good in America: Business and Politics Annual Study 2023," 2023, 6, https://globalstrategygroup .com/wp-content/uploads/2012/07/GSG-Business-and-Politics-Report-2023.pdf.

86. Rumstadt and Kanbach, "CEO Activism," 319. See also Melissa D. Dodd and Dustin W. Supa, "Conceptualizing and Measuring 'Corporate Social Advocacy' Communication: Examining the Impact on Corporate Financial Performance," *Public Relations Journal* 8, no. 3 (January 2014): 2, https://www.researchgate.net/pro file/Melissa-Dodd/publication/281005635_Conceptualizing_and_Measuring_Co rporate_Social_Advocacy_Communication_Examining_the_Impact_on_Corporate

_Financial_Performance/links/55d0dedb08aee19936fda2a8/Conceptualizing-and
-Measuring-Corporate-Social-Advocacy-Communication-Examining-the-Impact-on
-Corporate-Financial-Performance.pdf.

87. Global Strategy Group, "Shifting Politics," 7. See also Larcker et al., "Double-Edged Sword," 4, which found in 2018 that 35 percent of the public could think of a product or service they used *less* as a result of a position they didn't agree with, while only 20 percent could think of a product they used *more*.

88. Axios Harris Poll 100 results as reported in Eleanor Hawkins, "By the Numbers: Speaking Out," *Axios Communicators* email newsletter, June 22, 2023.

89. Jennifer Tonti, "JUST Capital's 2022 Americans' Views on Business Survey: Americans Want Less Talk, More Action," 2022, https://justcapital.com/reports/20 22-americans-views-on-business-survey/.

90. Lindsay Singleton, "Thinking: Navigating ESG in the New Congress," ROKK Solutions, Penn State Smeal College of Business, and Center for the Business of Sustainability, December 5, 2022, 11, https://rokksolutions.com/news/navigating -esg-in-the-new-congress/.

2. Shareholders and Stakeholders

Epigraph: Watson, *Business and Its Beliefs*, 78.

1. Mark Pendergrast, *For God, Country, and Coca-Cola: The Definitive History of the Great American Soft Drink and the Company That Makes It* (New York: Charles Scribner's Sons, 1993), 228.

2. Pendergrast, 273; and Herman E. Talmedge, *You and Segregation* (Marietta GA: The Truth At Last, 1955), 6, https://archive.org/details/YouAndSegregationBy HermanTalmadge/page/n1/mode/2up?view=theater.

3. Jeffrey Sonnenfeld, "The Great Business Retreat Matters in Russia Today—Just as It Mattered in 1986 South Africa," *Fortune*, March 7, 2022, https://fortune .com/2022/03/07/great-business-retreat-matters-russia-sanctions-1986-south-afri ca-putin-ukraine-world-politics-jeffrey-sonnenfeld/.

4. Watson, *Business and Its Beliefs*, 101.

5. Watson, 80.

6. Conference Board, "Historical Overview: 90 Years of Commitment," Annual Report, 2006, https://www.conference-board.org/pdf_free/TCB_HistoryTimeLine .pdf.

7. "Industry Unites for Good of All," *New York Times*, November 16, 1916, 18, https://timesmachine.nytimes.com/timesmachine/1916/11/16/301935092.pdf.

8. Freeman, *Strategic Management*, 31.

9. Watson, *Business and Its Beliefs*, 104.

10. Berle and Means, *Modern Corporation*, 310–11.

11. Gardiner Means, "Implications of the Corporate Revolution in Economic Theory," in Berle and Means, xxxv.

12. See Jerry Flint, "Napalm Bid Lost, Dow Still Target," *New York Times*, November 23, 1969, 38, https://timesmachine.nytimes.com/timesmachine/1969/11 /23/89146468.html; "Napalm and the Dow Chemical Company," *American Expe-*

rience, Public Broadcasting Service, accessed October 2, 2022, https://www.pbs.org
/wgbh/americanexperience/features/two-days-in-october-dow-chemical-and-use
-napalm; and Jonathan Soffer, "The National Association of Manufacturers and the
Militarization of American Conservatism," *Business History Review* 75, no. 4 (Winter
2001): 775–805.

13. General Electric, "1970 Annual Report," *The General Electric Investor* 2, no. 1
(Spring 1971): 3–4, https://archive.org/details/generalelectriccompanyannualre
ports/generalelectric1970/page/n1/mode/2up.

14. "Fortune 500," *Fortune*, 1970, https://money.cnn.com/magazines/fortune
/fortune500_archive/full/1970/.

15. Friedman, "Friedman Doctrine."

16. Wowak, Busenbark, and Hambrick, "How Do Employees React?," 581.

17. Lewis F. Powell Jr., "Powell Memorandum: Attack on the Free Enterprise
System," August 23, 1971, https://scholarlycommons.law.wlu.edu/powellmemo/1/.

18. Jensen and Meckling, "Theory of the Firm."

19. John F. Welch Jr. and Jack A. Byrnes, *Jack: Straight from the Gut* (New York:
Warner Books, 2001), 84. See also David Gelles, *The Man Who Broke Capitalism:
How Jack Welch Gutted the Heartland and Crushed the Soul of Corporate America—
and How to Undo His Legacy* (New York: Simon & Schuster, 2022) 38.

20. Francesco Guerrera, "Welch Condemns Share Price Focus," *Financial Times*,
March 12, 2009, https://www.ft.com/content/294ff1f2-0f27-11de-ba10-0000779f
d2ac.

21. Randall Poe, "Fast Forward," *Across the Board* 22, no. 12 (December 1985): 4.

22. David Ehrlich, in discussion with the author, July 5, 2022.

23. Sonnenfeld, *Corporate Views*, 1.

24. Council of Europe, *The European Social Charter: Collected Texts*, 7th ed., up-
dated January 2015, 9, https://rm.coe.int/CoERMPublicCommonSearchServices
/DisplayDCTMContent?documentId=090000168048b059. I am grateful to Julie
Battilana for this insight.

25. Temasek Holdings, "The Temasek Charter," accessed July 3, 2022, https://
www.temasekreview.com.sg/overview/the-temasek-charter.html.

26. Business Roundtable, "Statement on Corporate Responsibility," 1, 14.

27. Business Roundtable, "About Us," accessed July 30, 2022, https://www.bus
inessroundtable.org/about-us. The spring 1978 entry on a time-line history of the
Business Roundtable cites efforts to defeat "the creation of a large, overreaching
Consumer Protection Agency bureaucracy" and "an anti-business bill."

28. Jeffrey Sonnenfeld, in discussion with the author, July 29, 2022.

29. See, for instance, the characterization of the Friedmanite position as "funda-
mentalist" in Preston and Post, *Private Management and Public Policy*, 39.

30. Freeman, *Strategic Management*, 31.

31. Freeman, 241.

32. Mitchell, Agle, and Wood, "Toward a Theory of Stakeholder Identification,"
584.

33. Schwab with Vanham, *Stakeholder Capitalism*. Schwab first wrote about
stakeholder management in a paper published the same year that he founded the

precursor to the World Economic Forum. See Klaus Schwab and Hein Kroos, *Modern Company Management in Mechanical Engineering* (Frankfurt: Verein Deutscher Maschinenbau-Anstalten e.V., 1971).

34. Goodman, *Davos Man*, 37–45.

35. Business Roundtable, "Statement on Corporate Governance," September 1997, https://cdn.theconversation.com/static_files/files/693/Statement_on_Corporate_Governance_Business-Roundtable-1997%281%29.pdf?1566830902.

36. Englander and Kaufman, "End of Managerial Ideology."

37. I am grateful to Jeffrey Sonnenfeld for his insights about this.

38. Dave Kansas, "Goldman Chief's Reform Push Should Start Closer to Home," *Wall Street Journal*, June 11, 2002, https://www.wsj.com/articles/SB102374413762546040.

39. The Corporate and Auditing Accountability, Responsibility and Transparency Act of 2002: Hearings on H.R. 3763, March 20, 2002, before the House Committee on Financial Services, 107th Cong. 204 (2002) ("Statement of the Business Roundtable on the Corporate and Auditing Accountability, Responsibility and Transparency Act of 2002 (H.R. 3763) for the Committee on Financial Services, U.S. House of Representatives"), 352–59, https://www.google.com/books/edition/H_R_3763_the_Corporate_and_Auditing_Acco/WIi9i55fCOQC?hl=en&gbpv=1&dq=%E2%80%9CStatement+of+the+Business+Roundtable+on+the+Corporate+and+Auditing+Accountability,+Responsibility+and+Transparency+Act+of+2002+(H.R.+3763)+for+the+Committee+on+Financial+Services,+U.S.+House+of+Representatives%E2%80%9D&pg=PA351&printsec=frontcover.

40. Andrew Dugan, "Americans Still More Confident in Small vs. Big Business," Gallup, July 6, 2015, https://news.gallup.com/poll/183989/americans-confident-small-big-business.aspx.

41. Deborah Solomon and Serena Ng, "Fresh Pay Skirmish Erupts at AIG," *Wall Street Journal*, December 7, 2009, https://www.wsj.com/articles/SB126015238193279485; and Matt Phillips, "Goldman Sachs' Blankfein on Banking: 'Doing God's Work,'" *Wall Street Journal*, November 9, 2009, https://www.wsj.com/articles/BL-MB-13358.

42. Michael Dimock, "Defining Generations: Where Millennials End and Generation Z Begins," Pew Research Center, January 17, 2019, https://www.pewresearch.org/fact-tank/2019/01/17/where-millennials-end-and-generation-z-begins/.

43. Marlatt, "What Consumers Expect from CEOs," 6.

44. IBM100, "Building an Equal Opportunity, Workforce," accessed October 13, 2022, https://www.ibm.com/ibm/history/ibm100/us/en/icons/equalworkforce/transform/; and Associated Press, "Disney Co. Will Offer Benefits to Gay Partners," *New York Times*, October 8, 1995, https://www.nytimes.com/1995/10/08/us/disney-co-will-offer-benefits-to-gay-partners.html#:~:text=The%20Walt%20Disney%20Company%20will,companies%20to%20do%20the%20same.

45. Freedom to Marry, "Corporations and Businesses Stand for the Freedom to Marry," June 5, 2012, http://www.freedomtomarry.org/blog/entry/corporations-and-businesses-stand-for-the-freedom-to-marry.

46. Erik Eckholm, "Corporate Call for Change in Gay Marriage Case," *New York*

Times, February 27, 2013, https://www.nytimes.com/2013/02/28/business/compan ies-ask-justices-to-overturn-gay-marriage-ban.html.

47. Matt DeLong, "Google: 'Legalize Love' Campaign Isn't about Gay Marriage," *Washington Post*, July 8, 2012, https://www.washingtonpost.com/blogs/innovations /post/google-legalize-love-campaign-isnt-about-gay-marriage/2012/07/08/gJQAN 3PQWW_blog.html.

48. Starbucks Corporation, "Starbucks' CEO Hosts 2013 Annual Meeting of Shareholders Conference (Transcript)," Seeking Alpha, March 21, 2013, https://see kingalpha.com/article/1291061-starbucks-ceo-hosts-2013-annual-meeting-of-share holders-conference-transcript.

49. Starbucks stock price March 20, 2013, to January 15, 2023: Macrotrends, "Starbucks—31 Year Stock Price History," https://www.macrotrends.net/stocks /charts/SBUX/starbucks/stock-price-history.

50. Bryan Chaffin, "Tim Cook Soundly Rejects Politics of the NCPPR, Suggests Group Sell Apple's Stock," *The Mac Observer*, February 28, 2014, https://www.mac observer.com/tmo/article/tim-cook-soundly-rejects-politics-of-the-ncppr-suggests -group-sell-apples-s.

51. Apple reported a market cap of $434.1 billion to the Securities and Exchange Commission as of the end of 2013. See Apple, Inc., "Proxy Statement for 2014 Annual Meeting of Shareholders General Information," United States Securities and Exchange Commission, Schedule 14A, January 2014, https://www.sec.gov/Archives /edgar/data/320193/000119312513486406/d648739dpre14a.htm. Apple's market cap at the end of the first quarter of 2023 was $2.6 trillion. See also Nicholas Vega, "Tim Cook Became CEO of Apple 10 Years Ago. Here's How Much Money You'd Have if You Invested $1,000 in the Tech Giant the Day He Took Over," CNBC, August 24, 2021, https://www.cnbc.com/2021/08/24/how-much-apple-stock-has -grown-since-tim-cook-became-ceo-in-2011.html.

52. Bergh, interview by Tett, 9:09–9:32.

53. Business Roundtable, "Purpose of a Corporation."

54. See, for instance, David Benoit, "Move over Shareholders: Top CEOs See a Duty to Society," *Wall Street Journal*, August 19, 2019, https://www.wsj.com /articles/business-roundtable-steps-back-from-milton-friedman-theory-1156620 5200; David Gelles and David Yaffe-Bellany, "Feeling Heat, C.E.O.s Pledge New Priorities," *New York Times*, August 19, 2019, https://www.nytimes.com/2019/08 /19/business/business-roundtable-ceos-corporations.html; and Andrew Ross Sorkin, "How Shareholder Democracy Failed the People," *New York Times*, August 20, 2019, https://www.nytimes.com/2019/08/20/business/dealbook/business -roundtable-corporate-responsibility.html.

55. Lucian A. Bebchuk and Roberto Tallarita, "The Illusory Promise of Stake-holder Governance," *Cornell Law Review* 106 (2020): 91, http://dx.doi.org/10.2139 /ssrn.3544978.

56. Chirag Lala and Lenore Palladino, "Shareholders First: What Hasn't Changed since the Business Roundtable's 2019 Statement," *Roosevelt Institute*, August 19, 2020, https://rooseveltinstitute.org/2020/08/19/shareholders-first-what-hasnt -changed-since-the-business-roundtables-2019-statement/.

57. Bronagh Ward et al., "COVID-19 and Inequality: A Test of Corporate Purpose," KKS Advisors and Test of Corporate Purpose, September 2020, 43, https://c6a26163-5098-4e74-89da-9f6c9cc2e20c.filesusr.com/ugd/f64551_a55c15bb348f444982bfd28a030feb3c.pdf.

58. Venkataraman et al., "Making Business Do Better."

59. Means, "Implications of the Corporate Revolution," in Berle and Means, *Modern Corporation*, xxxv.

3. Filling the Void

1. Jeffrey M. Jones, "Confidence in U.S. Institutions Down; Average at New Low," Gallup, July 5, 2022, https://news.gallup.com/poll/394283/confidence-institutions-down-average-new-low.aspx. See also Gallup, "In Depth: Topics A to Z: Confidence in Institutions," accessed December 1, 2022, http://www.gallup.com/poll/1597/confidence-institutions.aspx.

2. Watson, *Business and Its Beliefs*, 101; and Pew Research Center, "Public Trust in Government: 1958–2023," September 19, 2023, https://www.pewresearch.org/politics/2023/09/19/public-trust-in-government-1958-2023/.

3. Pew Research Center, "Public Trust in Government."

4. Pew Research Center.

5. Robert D. Putnam, *Bowling Alone: The Collapse and Revival of American Community* (New York: Simon & Schuster, 2000).

6. Ilyse Hogue and Ellie Langford, *The Lie That Binds* (Washington DC: Strong Arm Press, 2020); Naomi Oreskes and Erik M. Conway, *Merchants of Doubt: How a Handful of Scientists Obscured the Truth on Issues from Tobacco Smoke to Climate Change* (New York: Bloomsbury Press, 2010); and Dave Lee, "Facebook Uncovers 'Russian-Funded' Misinformation Campaign," BBC, September 7, 2017, https://www.bbc.com/news/technology-41182519.

7. Edelman, *Trust in the Workplace*, 5.

8. Katie Couric, "Lessons from Afghanistan, the California Recall, and This Week's Friend of *Pivot* Is Nathan Allebach, aka the Steak-umm Twitter Guy," interview by Kara Swisher and Scott Galloway, *Pivot*, Vox Media, episode 231, August 31, 2021, 51:44.

9. Edelman, *2023 Edelman Trust Barometer: Global Report* (Edelman, 2023), 11, https://www.edelman.com/sites/g/files/aatuss191/files/2023-01/2023%20Edelman%20Trust%20Barometer%20Global%20Report.pdf.

10. Michelle Rodriguez, in discussion with the author, January 11, 2023.

11. Edelman, *2023 Global Report*, 41, 43, 29.

12. Edelman, 32.

13. Paul Polman, "CEOs Are Increasingly Stuck between Employees and Politicians. We Should Side with Our People," *Fortune*, May 16, 2022, https://fortune.com/2022/05/16/ceo-leadership-employees-politics-social-responsibility-buffalo-roe-wade-russia-environment-esg-human-rights-business-paul-polman/.

14. Edelman, *2022 Edelman Trust Barometer: The Changing Role of the Corporation in Society, Special Analysis Based on the 2022 Edelman Trust Barometer 2022 May*

Update (Edelman 2022), 22, https://www.hbs.edu/bigs/Shared%20Documents/20 22%20Edelman%20Trust%20Barometer%20Special%20Analysis%20Role%20 of%20Business%20BIGs.pdf.

15. Pew Research Center, "As Partisan Hostility Grows."

16. Conference Board, "Corporate America Faces Challenging Political Environment," February 7, 2023, https://www.conference-board.org/press/pressdetail.cfm ?pressid=19951.

17. Gelles, "Whole Foods Founder."

18. Conference Board, "Corporate America."

19. Mehta, "'It Was Not an Issue.'"

20. Tonti, "2021 Americans' Views on Business Survey."

21. Global Strategy Group, "Doing Business in an Activist World: 6th Annual Business & Politics Study," 2019, 8, https://globalstrategygroup.com/wp-content /uploads/2019/02/GSG-2019_Doing-Business-in-an-Activist-World_Business-and -Politics.pdf.

22. Sara Fischer, "The Brands that Transcend Politics," *Axios*, May 26, 2022, https://www.axios.com/2022/05/26/brands-politics-axios-harris-poll-100.

23. Edelman, *2023 Edelman Trust Barometer: Global Report* (Edelman, 2023), 28, https://www.edelman.com/sites/g/files/aatuss191/files/2023-01/2023%20Edel man%20Trust%20Barometer%20Global%20Report.pdf.

24. Black Rifle Coffee, "Who We Are," accessed March 1, 2023, https://www.black riflecoffee.com/pages/who-we-are; David Gelles, "Red Brands and Blue Brands: Is Hyper-Partisanship Coming for Corporate America?," *New York Times*, November 23, 2021, https://www.nytimes.com/2021/11/23/business/dealbook/companies -politics-partisan.html; and Jeremy's Razors, "We Value Truth and the Right to Speak It," accessed March 1, 2023, https://www.jeremysrazors.com/pages/about.

25. Not unlike current attacks by upstart brands like Jeremy's on "woke" businesses, then-independent Ben & Jerry's created a David-and-Goliath narrative about corporate rival Pillsbury with its "What's the Doughboy Afraid Of?" bumper sticker campaign in the mid-1980s. See Fred "Chico" Lager, *Ben & Jerry's: The Inside Scoop* (New York: Crown Publishing, 1994), 106–20. It also debuted Rainforest Crunch ice cream in 1989 to tout its commitment to biodiversity. See Edward O. Welles, "Ben's Big Flop," *Inc.*, September 1, 1998, https://www.inc.com/magazine/19980 901/995.html.

26. Bethany Biron and Heather Schlitz, "16 of the Biggest Controversies in Hobby Lobby's 50-Year History—from Denying Contraceptives for Employees to Illegally Smuggling Ancient Tablets," *Business Insider*, October 21, 2022, https:// www.businessinsider.com/the-15-biggest-controversies-in-hobby-lobby-history-20 20-9; and Axios Harris Poll, "The 2022 Axios Harris Poll 100 Reputation Rankings," *Axios*, May 24, 2022, https://www.axios.com/2022/05/24/2022-axios-harris-poll -100-rankings.

27. Axios Harris Poll, "The 2023 Axios Harris Poll 100 Reputation Rankings," *Axios*, May 23, 2023, https://www.axios.com/2023/05/23/corporate-brands-reputa tion-america.

28. Patagonia, "Earth Is Now Our Only Shareholder," accessed March 2, 2023,

https://www.patagonia.com/ownership/. Chouinard's letter is not dated, but it was reported in the *New York Times* on September 14, 2022. See David Gelles, "Billionaire No More: Patagonia Founder Gives Away the Company," *New York Times*, September 14, 2022, updated September 21, 2022, https://www.nytimes.com/2022/09/14/climate/patagonia-climate-philanthropy-chouinard.html.

29. Angus M. Thuermer Jr., "Patagonia Dumps Jackson Hole Ski Resort after Far-Right Fundraiser," *Wyofile*, August 18, 2021, https://www.wyofile.com/patagonia-dumps-jackson-hole-ski-resort-after-far-right-fundraiser/.

30. Fos, Kempf, and Tsoutsoura, "Political Polarization," 27.

31. Ramaswamy, *Woke, Inc.*

32. Shubhashis Gangopadhyay and Swarnodeep HomRoy, "Strategic CEO Activism in Polarized Markets," June 1, 2020, 18, 25, updated January 2021, http://dx.doi.org/10.2139/ssrn.3622605.

33. Jeffrey Sonnenfeld, "People Trust Executives to Intervene in Social Issues, Says Jeffrey Sonnenfeld," *The Economist*, September 14, 2022, https://www.economist.com/by-invitation/2022/09/14/people-trust-executives-to-intervene-in-social-issues-says-jeffrey-sonnenfeld.

34. Marc Benioff (@benioff), "We are forced to dramatically reduce our investment in IN based on our employee's & customer's outrage over the Religious Freedom Bill," Twitter, March 25, 2015, 9:32 p.m., https://twitter.com/Benioff/status/580905037162885121. See also Benioff (@benioff), "Today we are canceling all programs that require our customers/employees to travel to Indiana to face discrimination," Twitter, March 26, 2015, 11:02 a.m., https://twitter.com/Benioff/status/581108959337136129.

35. Mark Peters and Ashby Jones, "Indiana Lawmakers Move to Clarify Religious-Objections Law," *Wall Street Journal*, March 30, 2015, https://www.wsj.com/articles/indiana-lawmakers-move-to-clarify-religious-objections-law-1427726920.

36. Alexander C. Kaufman, "More than 70 Tech Execs Sign 'Historic' Statement against LGBT Discrimination," *HuffPost*, April 1, 2015, updated April 2, 2015, https://www.huffpost.com/entry/tech-executives-lgbt_n_6986654.

37. Eugene Kim, "Salesforce Wrote a $50,000 Check to Move an Employee out of Indiana," *Business Insider*, April 2, 2015, https://www.businessinsider.com/salesforce-offers-indiana-employee-relocation-package-2015-4.

38. Human Rights Campaign and Equality North Carolina, "Letter to North Carolina Governor McCrory," accessed November 28, 2022, https://assets2.hrc.org/files/assets/resources/NC_CEO_Letter_(3).pdf.

39. Jon Swartz and Elizabeth Weise, "PayPal Withdraws Planned N.C. Expansion due to Anti-Gay Law," *USA Today*, April 5, 2016, https://www.usatoday.com/story/tech/news/2016/04/05/paypal-withdraws-planned-nc-expansion-due-anti-gay-law/82649786/.

40. Dan Schulman, "PayPal Withdraws Plan for Charlotte Expansion," PayPal Newsroom, April 5, 2016, https://newsroom.paypal-corp.com/PayPal-Withdraws-Plan-for-Charlotte-Expansion.

41. Wowak, Busenbark, and Hambrick, "How Do Employees React?," 554. For the source data cited in this analysis, see SurveyUSA, "Results of SurveyUSA Elec-

tion Poll #22836: NC Voters Continue to Wrestle with HB2 Fallout: Majority in State Now Opposes New 'Bathroom' Law in General, but Supports Specific Birth-Gender Provision," 2016, https://www.surveyusa.com/client/PollReport.aspx?g=7fa42c9f -a1bc-4cee-b3a4-26c8cd2c3a40.

42. *State of Washington et al. v. Donald J. Trump et al.*; and Nyshka Chandran, "Intel CEO Brian Krzanich Quits Trump's Manufacturing Council," CNBC, August 14, 2017, https://www.cnbc.com/2017/08/14/intel-ceo-quit-trumps-manufacturing -council.html.

43. "Full Transcript and Video: Trump's News Conference in New York," *New York Times*, August 15, 2017, https://www.nytimes.com/2017/08/15/us/politics /trump-press-conference-transcript.html; and Sheryl Gay Stolberg and Brian M. Rosenthal, "Man Charged after White Nationalist Rally in Charlottesville Ends in Deadly Violence," *New York Times*, August 12, 2017, https://www.nytimes.com/2017 /08/12/us/charlottesville-protest-white-nationalist.html.

44. Kenneth C. Frazier (@Merck), "Statement from Kenneth C. Frazier, chairman and chief executive officer, Merck," Twitter, August 14, 2017, 8:00 a.m., https:// twitter.com/Merck/status/897065338566791169. The full statement follows: "I am resigning from the President's American Manufacturing Council. Our country's strength stems from its diversity and the contributions made by men and women of different faiths, races, sexual orientations and political beliefs. America's leaders must honor our fundamental values by clearly rejecting expressions of hatred, bigotry, and group supremacy, which run counter to the American ideal that all people are created equal. As CEO of Merck and as a matter of personal conscience, I feel a responsibility to stand against intolerance and extremism."

45. Chandran, "Intel CEO Brian Krzanich."

46. Lucy Bayly, Haley Messenger, and Emily Pandise, "CEOs and Business Leaders Condemn 'Appalling Events' at Capitol, Push for Unity," CNBC, January 6, 2021, https://www.nbcnews.com/business/business-news/ceos-business-leaders-conde mn-appalling-events-capitol-push-unity-n1253161; and Alex Gangitano, "Here Are the Companies Suspending Political Contributions Following the Capitol Riots," *The Hill*, 1/21/21, https://thehill.com/business-a-lobbying/533795-here-are-the-com panies-suspending-political-contributions-following-the/.

47. Nathan Layne, "Explainer: Big Changes under Georgia's New Election Law," *Reuters*, June 14, 2021, https://www.reuters.com/world/us/big-changes-under-geor gias-new-election-law-2021-06-14/.

48. Marc Benioff (@benioff), "A person's right to cast their ballot is the foundation of our democracy. Georgia HB 531 would limit trustworthy, safe & equal access to voting by restricting early voting & eliminating provisional ballots. That's why Salesforce opposes HB 531 as it stands. #gapol 🗳️," Twitter, March 16, 2021, 7:27 p.m., https://twitter.com/Benioff/status/1371966423682084864. See also Brad Smith (@BradSmi), "A healthy democracy needs all voices to be heard and a number of proposed bills in Georgia as drafted will restrict fair and secure elections. We are joining other business leaders in Georgia to support all eligible citizens' right to vote," Twitter, March 22, 2021, 2:55 p.m., https://twitter.com/BradSmi/status/13 74072187263533057.

49. Kenneth Chenault et al., "Memo to Corporate America: The Fierce Urgency Is Now," *New York Times* (advertisement), A7, March 31, 2021, https://a9p9n2x2.sta ckpathcdn.com/wp-content/blogs.dir/1/files/2021/03/BEA_3.31-E-Etear.pdf.

50. Andrew Ross Sorkin and David Gelles, "Black Executives Call on Corporations to Fight Restrictive Voting Laws," *New York Times*, March 31, 2021, updated April 3, 2021, https://www.nytimes.com/2021/03/31/business/voting-rights-geor gia-corporations.html.

51. David Shepardson and Uday Sampath Kumar, "Delta, Coca-Cola Blast Home State Georgia's Voting Restrictions as 'Unacceptable,'" Reuters, March 31, 2021, https://www.reuters.com/article/us-usa-georgia-voting-companies-idUSKBN2B N1M9.

52. Madhu Unnikrishnan, "Delta Nearly Loses Tax Benefit in Georgia over Elections Law Retribution," *Airline Weekly*, April 1, 2021, https://airlineweekly.com/2021 /04/delta-nearly-loses-tax-benefit-in-georgia-over-elections-law-retribution/.

53. Kevin Draper et al., "M.L.B. Pulls All-Star Game from Georgia in Response to Voting Law," *New York Times*, April 3, 2021, updated April 6, 2021, https://www.ny times.com/2021/04/02/us/politics/mlb-all-star-game-moved-atlanta-georgia.html.

54. Natasha Dailey, "Meet the Team of Black Executives Who Quickly Mobilized Hundreds of CEOs to Oppose Restrictive Voting Laws," *Business Insider*, April 15, 2021, https://www.businessinsider.com/restrictive-voting-laws-companies-ceos-ad -organized-by-black-executives-2021-4.

55. Texas Senate bill 1, "Relating to Election Integrity and Security, Including by Preventing Fraud in the Conduct of Elections in This State; Increasing Criminal Penalties; Creating Criminal Offenses, Providing Civil Penalties," 2021, https://cap itol.texas.gov/tlodocs/871/billtext/pdf/SB00001I.pdf.

56. Fair Elections Texas, "Fair Elections Texas," accessed January 3, 2023, https:// www.fairelectionstexas.org/fair-elections-texas-letter.pdf.

57. Swarnodeep HomRoy and Shubhashis Gangopadhyay, "PAC-ing a Punch: Economic Effects of Corporate Political Statements," June 2, 2021, http://dx.doi.org /10.2139/ssrn.3976194.

58. Citizens for Responsibility and Ethics in Washington, "This Sedition Is Brought to You by . . . ," June 23, 2021, https://www.citizensforethics.org/reports-in vestigations/crew-reports/this-sedition-is-brought-to-you-by/.

59. Hannah Hartig, "About Six-in-Ten Americans Say Abortion Should Be Legal in All or Most Cases," Pew Research Center, June 13, 2022, https://www.pewresear ch.org/fact-tank/2022/06/13/about-six-in-ten-americans-say-abortion-should-be -legal-in-all-or-most-cases-2/.

60. Neelam Bohra, "Texas Law Banning Abortion as Early as Six Weeks Goes into Effect as the U.S. Supreme Court Takes No Action," *Texas Tribune*, August 31, 2021, https://www.texastribune.org/2021/08/31/texas-abortion-law-supreme-court/.

61. Don't Ban Equality, "Don't Ban Equality in Texas," accessed January 4, 2023, https://dontbanequality.com/dont-ban-equality-2/.

62. Nadella, interview by Swisher and Galloway, 46:28–46:40.

63. Charles Riley, "Bumble and Match Pledge to Help People Affected by Texas Abortion Law," CNN Business, September 3, 2021, https://www.cnn.com/2021/09 /03/tech/match-bumble-texas-abortion-law/index.html.

64. Marc Benioff (@benioff), "Ohana if you want to move we'll help you exit TX. Your choice," Twitter, September 10, 2021, 9:54 p.m., https://twitter.com/Benioff/status/1436508394194718720.

65. Sandberg wrote, "This is a scary day for women all across our country. If the leaked draft opinion becomes the law of the land, one of our most fundamental rights will be taken away. Every woman, no matter where she lives, must be free to choose whether and when she becomes a mother. Few things are more important to women's health and equality." Sheryl Sandberg, Facebook, May 3, 2022, https://www.facebook.com/sheryl/posts/10166165694830177.

66. Unzipped Staff, "Protecting Reproductive Rights: A Business Imperative," Levi Strauss & Co. (blog), May 4, 2022, https://www.levistrauss.com/2022/05/04/protecting-reproductive-rights-a-business-imperative/.

67. Nelson Oliveira, "Bank of America CEO Calls Roe v. Wade 'Settled Law,' Says Company Will Discuss Providing Benefits to Employees Seeking an Abortion," CBS News, May 4, 2022, https://www.cbsnews.com/news/roe-v-wade-abortion-bank-of-america-ceo-brian-moynihan/. Moynihan's use of the phrase "settled law of the land" could be read as a variation on a talking point used by conservative Supreme Court nominees trying to avoid taking a stance on the issue. See Becky Sullivan, "What Conservative Justices Said—and Didn't Say—about Roe at Their Confirmations," NPR, May 3, 2022, updated June 24, 2022, https://www.npr.org/2022/05/03/1096108319/roe-v-wade-alito-conservative-justices-confirmation-hearings.

68. Pavithra Mohan and Julia Herbst, "Why Corporate America Is Afraid to Talk about Abortion," *Fast Company*, May 16, 2022, https://www.fastcompany.com/90751659/why-corporate-america-is-afraid-to-talk-about-abortion.

69. "Walmart Tells Employees It's Studying 'Best Path Forward' on Abortion," *Dallas Morning News*, July 2, 2022, https://www.dallasnews.com/business/retail/2022/07/02/walmart-tells-employees-its-studying-best-path-forward-on-abortion/.

70. Rhia Ventures, "#WhatAreYourReproBenefits," accessed March 14, 2023, https://rhiaventures.org/corporate-engagement/whatareyourreprobenefits/.

71. Caitlin Harrington, "Tech Companies Will Cover Abortion Travel—but Not for All Workers," *Wired*, July 7, 2022, https://www.wired.com/story/tech-companies-abortion-travel/.

72. Don't Ban Equality, "These Companies Stand with Don't Ban Equality," accessed March 23, 2022, https://dontbanequality.com/.

73. Conference Board, "The US Corporate Response to Recent Supreme Court Decisions," July 19, 2022, https://www.conference-board.org/topics/civil-just-society/US-corporate-response-to-Supreme-Court-decisions.

74. U.S. Food and Drug Administration, "Information about Mifepristone for Medical Termination of Pregnancy through Ten Weeks Gestation," March 23, 2023, https://www.fda.gov/drugs/postmarket-drug-safety-information-patients-and-providers/information-about-mifepristone-medical-termination-pregnancy-through-ten-weeks-gestation; and Missouri attorney general Andrew Bailey, "Attorney General Bailey Directs Letter to CVS and Walgreens over Distribution of Abortion Pills," February 1, 2023, https://ago.mo.gov/home/news/2023/02/01/attorney-general-bailey-directs-letter-to-cvs-and-walgreens-over-distribution-of-abortion-pills.

75. Kansas attorney general Kris W. Kobach, "AG Kris Kobach to Walgreens:

Follow the Law on Mail-Order Abortifacients," February 6, 2023, https://ag.ks.gov/media-center/news-releases/2023/02/06/ag-kris-kobach-to-walgreens-follow-the-law-on-mail-order-abortifacients.

76. Pam Belluck and Julie Creswell, "Walgreens Faces Blowback for Not Offering Abortion Pill in 21 States," *New York Times*, March 7, 2023, https://www.nytimes.com/2023/03/07/business/walgreens-abortion-pill.html.

77. Anjalee Khemlani, "Walgreens Internal Memo Says It Is Following the Law on Abortion Pill Distribution," Yahoo! Finance, March 7, 2023, https://news.yahoo.com/walgreens-internal-memo-says-it-is-following-the-law-on-abortion-pill-distribution-201906683.html.

78. Karen Lynch, interview by Hope King, Axios What's Next Summit, Washington, DC, March 29, 2023.

79. National Aeronautics and Space Administration, "Scientific Consensus: Earth's Climate Is Warming," accessed March 8, 2023, https://climate.nasa.gov/scientific-consensus/.

80. Juliet Eilperin, "Obama Unveils Ambitious Agenda to Combat Climate Change, Bypassing Congress," *Washington Post*, June 25, 2013, https://www.washingtonpost.com/politics/obama-climate-strategy-represents-piecemeal-approach/2013/06/25/7bd9f20a-dd0a-11e2-bd83-e99e43c336ed_story.html; and Coral Davenport, "What Trump Can and Can't Do to Dismantle Obama's Climate Rules," *New York Times*, January 26, 2017, https://www.nytimes.com/2017/01/26/us/politics/donald-trump-climate-epa.html.

81. David Gelles, "Corner Office: How Panera Bread Navigated Covid, the Labor Market, Inflation and More," *New York Times*, April 15, 2022, https://www.nytimes.com/2022/04/15/business/panera-niren-chaudhary-corner-office.html.

82. Bill Weihl, "ClimateVoices Featuring Paul Polman (AKA "Captain Planet")," LinkedIn, October 4, 2022, https://www.linkedin.com/pulse/climatevoices-featuring-paul-polman-aka-captain-planet-bill-weihl.

83. Mark Tercek, "Corporate Climate Efforts Are Not Greenwashing but . . . They Need Public Policy to Succeed," *The Instigator*, June 5, 2022, https://marktercek.substack.com/p/corporate-climate-efforts-are-not.

84. Tim Cook, "The Legacy of Steve Jobs, at Code 2022," interview by Kara Swisher and Scott Galloway, *Pivot*, Vox Media, September 28, 2022, 18:55–19:30.

85. Jim Snyder, "Apple Leaves U.S. Chamber over Stance on Climate Change Bill," *The Hill*, October 6, 2009, https://thehill.com/homenews/news/51713-apple-leaves-u-s-chamber-over-stance-on-climate-change-bill/#:~:text=Apple%20announced%20Monday%20it%20would,the%20Chamber%20over%20global%20warming.

86. Kenza Bryan, "COP27: Mark Carney Clings to His Dream of a Greener Finance Industry," *Financial Times*, November 9, 2022, https://www.ft.com/content/8d0c1064-881e-42b4-9075-18e646f3e1ad.

87. Tercek, "Corporate Climate Efforts."

88. Jason R. Silva, "Global Mass Shootings: Comparing the United States against Developed and Developing Countries," *International Journal of Comparative and Applied Criminal Justice*, 2022, https://doi.org/10.1080/01924036.2022.2052126; and Katherine Leach-Kemon and Rebecca Sirull, "On Gun Violence, the

United States Is an Outlier," University of Washington School of Medicine, the Institute for Health Metrics and Evaluation (IHME), May 31, 2022, https://www.healthdata.org/acting-data/gun-violence-united-states-outlier.

89. Schultz, "Our Respectful Request."

90. CEOs for Gun Safety, "2022 Signatories," accessed February 15, 2023, https://www.ceosforgunsafety.org/pages/2022.

4. The Empire Strikes Back

1. Texas SB 13, Chapter 809, "Prohibition on Investment in Financial Companies that Boycott Certain Energy Companies," 2021, https://capitol.texas.gov/tlodo cs/87R/billtext/pdf/SB00013F.pdf#navpanes=0.

2. West Virginia SB 262, Article 1C, "Financial Institutions Engaged in Boycotts of Energy Companies," 2022, https://www.wvlegislature.gov/Bill_Status/bil ls_text.cfm?billdoc=SB262%20SUB2%20ENR.htm&yr=2022&sesstype=RS&billt ype=B&houseorig=S&i=262; Kentucky SB 205, "An Act Relating to State Dealings with Companies That Engage in Energy Company Boycotts," 2022, https://apps.legisl ature.ky.gov/record/22rs/SB205.html; and Oklahoma SB 1572, "Energy Discrimination Elimination Act," 2022, http://oklegislature.gov/cf_pdf/2021-22%20INT/sb /SB1572%20int.pdf.

3. West Virginia state treasurer Riley Moore, "Treasurer Moore Publishes Restricted Financial Institution List," July 28, 2022, https://www.wvtreasury.com /About-The-Office/Press-Releases/ID/452/Treasurer-Moore-Publishes-Restricted -Financial-Institution-List.

4. Banking on Climate Chaos, "Banking on Climate Chaos: Fossil Fuel Finance Report 2022," March 30, 2022, https://www.bankingonclimatechaos.org//wp-con tent/themes/bocc-2021/inc/bcc-data-2022/BOCC_2022_vSPREAD.pdf.

5. Nadia Kähkönen, Elliott Bourgeault, and Isabel Hagbrink, *Net Zero and Beyond: A Deep-Dive on Climate Leaders and What's Driving Them* (South Pole, October 18, 2022), 4, https://www.southpole.com/news/going-green-then-going-dark.

6. Texas SB 19, "Relating to Prohibited Contracts with Companies that Discriminate against the Firearm or Ammunition Industries," 2021, https://capitol.texas .gov/tlodocs/87R/billtext/pdf/SB00019F.pdf.

7. Gandel, "Texas Law That Has Banks Saying."

8. Daniel Garrett and Ivan Ivanov, "Gas, Guns, and Governments: Financial Costs of Anti-ESG Policies," Jacobs Levy Equity Management Center for Quantitative Financial Research Paper, May 30, 2022, last revised February 23, 2023, http:// dx.doi.org/10.2139/ssrn.4123366.

9. Econsult Solutions, Inc., "ESG Boycott Legislation in States: Municipal Bond Market Impact," January 12, 2023, http://econsultsolutions.com/esg-boycott-legisla tion-municipal-bond-impact.

10. Krista Buckel, "Attorney General Cameron Announces Multi-State Investigation into Six Major Banks for ESG Investment Practices," October 19, 2022, https:// www.kentucky.gov/Pages/Activity-stream.aspx?n=AttorneyGeneral&prId=1269; and Hope of Kentucky, LLC, and Kentucky Bankers Association v. Daniel Cameron, in his official capacity as the attorney general of the Commonwealth of Kentucky,

"Complaint for Declaration of Rights and for Injunctive Relief," Commonwealth of Kentucky Franklin Circuit Court, October 31, 2022, 11, 4, https://www.kybanks.com/kba-files/pdf/comleg/2022_10_31_HOPE_KBA_Complaint_vs_AGCameron_CIDs_22CI842_AsFiled.pdf.

11. Don Lee, "Disney's Health Benefits for Gays Draws Protest: Insurance: 15 Florida Legislators Send Letter to Company, Which Declines to Respond. Analysts Discount Concerns," Los Angeles Times, October 19, 1995, https://www.latimes.com/archives/la-xpm-1995-10-19-fi-58834-story.html.

12. Sue Anne Pressley, "Apple Rebuffed in Texas over Gay Benefits Policy," Washington Post, December 1, 1993, https://www.washingtonpost.com/archive/business/1993/12/01/apple-rebuffed-in-texas-over-gay-benefits-policy/576ca14d-111a-4578-aa5d-2ff6d3248d2d/; and Sam Howe Verhovek, "Texas County Retreats over Apple's Gay Policy," New York Times, December 8, 1993, https://www.nytimes.com/1993/12/08/us/texas-county-retreats-over-apple-s-gay-policy.html.

13. David Bowdich, acting deputy director, Federal Bureau of Investigation, Statement before the House Judiciary Committee, "Summary and Timeline Related to Parkland Shooting Investigation: Statement for the Record," Washington DC, March 20, 2018, https://www.fbi.gov/news/testimony/summary-and-timeline-related-to-parkland-shooting-investigation; and WSBTV.com, "Delta Latest Company Ending Discounts, Benefits for NRA Members," Atlanta Journal-Constitution, February 25, 2018, https://www.ajc.com/news/delta-ending-discount-for-nra-members/udsVbUxN560QS2n79yuc6K/.

14. Daniel Uria, "Georgia Lawmakers Pass Tax Bill without Delta Break," U.S. News, March 1, 2018, https://www.upi.com/Top_News/US/2018/03/01/Georgia-lawmakers-pass-tax-bill-without-Delta-break/6891519951582/.

15. Bart Jansen, "Delta Airlines NRA Dispute: Only 13 Passengers Ever Bought Tickets," USA Today, March 2, 2018, https://www.usatoday.com/story/news/2018/03/02/delta-reviews-all-fare-discount-programs-after-nra-dispute-costs-georgia-tax-break/388587002/.

16. Julie Creswell and Michael Corkery, "Walmart and Dick's Raise Minimum Age for Gun Buyers to 21," New York Times, February 28, 2018, https://www.nytimes.com/2018/02/28/business/walmart-and-dicks-major-gun-retailers-will-tighten-rules-on-guns-they-sell.html.

17. Ed Skyler, "Announcing Our U.S. Commercial Firearms Policy," Citi, March 22, 2018, https://www.citigroup.com/global/news/perspective/2018/announcing-our-us-commercial-firearms-policy.

18. Tiffany Hsu, "Citigroup Sets Restrictions on Gun Sales by Business Partners," New York Times, March 22, 2018, https://www.nytimes.com/2018/03/22/business/citigroup-gun-control-policy.html.

19. Erin A. Catlett, "Banks and Guns: Social Activism Following the Parkland, Florida Shooting," North Carolina Banking Institute Journal 23 (2019): 507, https://scholarship.law.unc.edu/ncbi/vol23/iss1/25. See also Laura J. Keller and Polly Mosendz, "BofA Will Stop Lending to Makers of Assault-Style Guns," Bloomberg, April 10, 2018, https://www.bloomberg.com/news/articles/2018-04-10/bofa-will-no-longer-lend-to-some-gunmakers-vice-chairman-says.

20. Conor Gibson and Frances Sawyer, *2023 Statehouse Report: Right-Wing Attacks on the Freedom to Invest Responsibly Falter in Legislatures* (Pleiades Strategy, 2023), 3, https://www.pleiadesstrategy.com/state-house-report-bill-tracker-republican-anti-esg-attacks-on-freedom-to-invest-responsibly-earns-business-labor-and-environmental-opposition.

21. Ropes & Gray, "Navigating State Regulation of ESG," accessed July 18, 2023, https://www.ropesgray.com/en/navigating-state-regulation-of-esg.

22. US 117th Congress, "H.R.7896—No ESG at TSP Act," introduced May 27, 2022, https://www.congress.gov/bill/117th-congress/house-bill/7896/text.

23. H.J. Resolution 30, 188th Congress, 1st session, February 7, 2023, https://www.congress.gov/118/bills/hjres30/BILLS-118hjres30ih.pdf; and Employee Benefits Security Administration, "Prudence and Loyalty in Selecting Plan Investments and Exercising Shareholder Rights," *Federal Register*, December 1, 2022, https://www.federalregister.gov/documents/2022/12/01/2022-25783/prudence-and-loyalty-in-selecting-plan-investments-and-exercising-shareholder-rights.

24. Ron DeSantis, "Governor Ron DeSantis Eliminates ESG Considerations from State Pension Investments," August 23, 2022, https://www.flgov.com/2022/08/23/governor-ron-desantis-eliminates-esg-considerations-from-state-pension-investments/.

25. Florida CFO Jimmy Patronis, Office of Communications, "IN CASE YOU MISSED IT . . . Bloomberg: 'Florida Escalates ESG War, Says BlackRock's Larry Fink "Did It to Himself,"'" December 15, 2022, https://myfloridacfo.com/news/pressreleases/prior-press-releases/archive-details/2023/09/20/in-case-you-missed-it-bloomberg-florida-escalates-esg-war-says-blackrock-s-larry-fink-did-it-to-himself.

26. Ron DeSantis, "Governor Ron DeSantis Signs Legislation to Protect Floridians from Discrimination and Woke Indoctrination," April 22, 2022, https://www.flgov.com/2022/04/22/governor-ron-desantis-signs-legislation-to-protect-floridians-from-discrimination-and-woke-indoctrination/.

27. *Honeyfund.com, Inc., et al. v. Ron DeSantis, in his official Capacity as Governor of Florida, et al.*, Preliminary Injunction, Case No. 4:22cv227-MW/MAF (US District Court Northern District of Florida, Tallahassee Division, August 18, 2022, https://aboutblaw.com/4xn.

28. Florida CS/CS/HB 155, "Parental Rights in Education," 2022, https://www.myfloridahouse.gov/Sections/Bills/billsdetail.aspx?BillId=76545.

29. Ramaswamy, *Woke, Inc.*, 63.

30. Brian Rokus, Kit Maher, and David Wright, "Vivek Ramaswamy Announces GOP Bid for President in 2024," CNN, February 21, 2023, https://www.cnn.com/2023/02/21/politics/vivek-ramaswamy-gop-2024-campaign/index.html.

31. John McWhorter, "How 'Woke' Became an Insult," *New York Times*, August 17, 2021, https://www.nytimes.com/2021/08/17/opinion/woke-politically-correct.html; and Google Trends search on "woke," January 1, 2004, to November 15, 2023, https://trends.google.com/trends/explore?date=all&geo=US&q=%2Fg%2F11ddxplprk.

32. Juliana Menasce Horowitz, "Support for Black Lives Matter Declined after George Floyd Protests, but Has Remained Unchanged Since," Pew Research Center,

September 27, 2021, https://www.pewresearch.org/fact-tank/2021/09/27/support
-for-black-lives-matter-declined-after-george-floyd-protests-but-has-remained-un
changed-since/. The Pew Research Center provided additional data confirming that
this trend has continued: in September 2020 (53 percent), September 2021 (50
percent), and March 2022 (49 percent), approximately half of white Americans said
they oppose Black Lives Matter.

33. Singleton, "Navigating ESG in the New Congress," 8.

34. Singleton, 1.

35. Letter from fourteen state financial officers to James Dimon, March 23,
2023, https://s.wsj.net/public/resources/documents/AGs-Letter-to-JP-Morgan
-Chase.pdf.

36. Letter from Kentucky attorney general Daniel Cameron et al. to Jamie Dimon, May 2, 2023, https://www.ag.ky.gov/Press%20Release%20Attachments/23
.5.2%20Letter%20to%20Chase.pdf.

37. See, for instance, Matt Walsh (@MattWalshBlog), "The goal is to make 'pride'
toxic for brands. If they decide to shove this garbage in our face, they should know
that they'll pay a price. It won't be worth whatever they think they'll gain. First
Bud Light and now Target. Our campaign is making progress. Let's keep it going,"
Twitter, May 24, 2023, 7:27 a.m., https://twitter.com/MattWalshBlog/status/16613
33191951613952.

38. Axios Harris Poll, "2022 Axios Harris Poll"; and Nikki McCann Ramirez,
"Not Even Chick-fil-A Is Safe from Anti-'Woke' Right Wingers," *Rolling Stone*, May
31, 2023, https://www.rollingstone.com/politics/politics-news/chick-fil-a-corporate
-diversity-policies-targets-conservatives-1234743961/.

39. Letter from Indiana attorney general Todd Rokita et al. to Brian Cornell,
CEO of Target Corporation, July 5, 2023, https://content.govdelivery.com/attachme
nts/INAG/2023/07/06/file_attachments/2546257/Target%20Letter%20Final.pdf.

40. Ron DeSantis (@GovRonDeSantis), "We've kneecapped ESG in Florida. So
I'm calling for an investigation into AB InBev's actions regarding their Bud Light
marketing campaign and falling stock prices. All options are on the table and woke
corporations that put ideology ahead of returns should be on notice," Twitter, July
21, 2023, 7:51 a.m., https://twitter.com/GovRonDeSantis/status/168235757170797
3635.

41. Human Rights Campaign, "Count Us In Pledge," accessed August 1, 2023,
https://www.hrc.org/resources/count-us-in-pledge.

42. Letter from Massachusetts attorney general Andrea Joy Campbell et al. to
Target CEO Brian Cornell, June 16, 2023, https://attorneygeneral.delaware.gov/wp
-content/uploads/sites/50/2023/06/Target-Pride-Letter-2023.06.16.pdf.

43. *Students for Fair Admissions, Inc., v. President and Fellows of Harvard College*, 600 U.S. __ (2023), https://www.supremecourt.gov/opinions/22pdf/20-1199
_hgdj.pdf.

44. Letter from Kansas attorney general Kris Kobach et al. to Fortune 100 CEOs,
July 13, 2023, https://ag.ks.gov/docs/default-source/documents/corporate-racial
-discrimination-multistate-letter.pdf?sfvrsn=968abc1a_2.

45. Letter from Senator Tom Cotton to Brian C. Cornell, CEO of Target, July 7,
2023, https://www.cotton.senate.gov/imo/media/doc/target_letter.pdf.

46. Ramaswamy, *Woke, Inc.*, 1.

47. Liz Hoffman and Charley Grant, "'Woke, Inc.' Author's Startup to Take on BlackRock," *Wall Street Journal*, May 10, 2022, https://www.wsj.com/articles/up start-money-manager-gets-billionaires-to-back-the-anti-blackrock-11652134919.

48. Consumers' Research, "About BlackRock," accessed February 26, 2023, https://consumersresearch.org/blackrock/.

49. Arizona attorney general Mark Brnovich, "Arizona Attorney General Mark Brnovich Calls Out Potentially Unlawful Market Manipulation by Investment Firm," August 4, 2022, https://www.azag.gov/press-release/arizona-attorney-gener al-mark-brnovich-calls-out-potentially-unlawful-market.

50. Lieutenant Governor of Texas Dan Patrick, "Letter to Comptroller Hegar to Place BlackRock at the Top of the List of Financial Companies That Boycott the Texas Oil & Gas Industry," January 19, 2022, https://www.ltgov.texas.gov/2022/01 /19/lt-gov-dan-patrick-letter-to-comptroller-hegar-to-place-blackrock-at-the-top-of -the-list-of-financial-companies-that-boycott-the-texas-oil-gas-industry/.

51. Letter from North Carolina state treasurer Dale Folwell to BlackRock direc- tors, December 9, 2022, https://www.nctreasurer.com/media/4255/download?atta chment.

52. Indiana Legislative Services Agency, Office of Fiscal and Management Analy- sis, "Fiscal Impact Statement, LS 6994, Bill Number: HB 1008," February 4, 2023.

53. US Energy Information Administration, "North Dakota State Energy Pro- file," last updated July 20, 2023, https://www.eia.gov/state/print.php?sid=ND; and North Dakota 68th Legislative Assembly (2023–25), HB 1347, February 1, 2023, https://www.ndlegis.gov/assembly/68-2023/regular/bill-overview/b01347.html.

54. Rob Kozlowski, "Chevron Taps BlackRock as Target-Date, Index Fund Man- ager for 401(k)," *Pensions & Investments*, July 10, 2023, https://www.pionline.com /searches-and-hires/chevron-taps-blackrock-target-date-index-fund-manager-401k.

55. Larry Fink, interview by Andrew Ross Sorkin, Dealbook Summit, New York, November 30, 2022, 13:42–13.45, https://www.youtube.com/watch?v=PSVpth7uqb4.

56. Lananh Nguyen and Simon Jessop, "Davos 2023: BlackRock U.S. Inflows Dwarf $4 Bln Lost in ESG Backlash—CEO," Reuters, January 17, 2023, https://www .reuters.com/business/finance/davos-2023-blackrock-us-inflows-dwarf-4-bln-lost -esg-backlash-ceo-2023-01-17/.

57. Larry Fink, "Larry Fink's Annual Chairman's Letter to Investors," BlackRock, accessed August 2, 2023, https://www.blackrock.com/corporate/investor-relations /larry-fink-annual-chairmans-letter; and Isla Binnie, "BlackRock's Fink Says He's Stopped Using 'Weaponised' Term ESG," Reuters, June 26, 2023, https://www .reuters.com/business/environment/blackrocks-fink-says-hes-stopped-usin g-weaponised-term-esg-2023-06-26/.

58. BlackRock Investment Stewardship, "2022 Climate-Related Shareholder Proposals More Prescriptive than 2021," May 2022, https://www.blackrock.com/co rporate/literature/publication/commentary-bis-approach-shareholder-proposals .pdf.

59. Brooke Masters, "BlackRock Opens Door for Retail Investors to Vote in Proxy Battles," *Financial Times*, November 2, 2022, https://www.ft.com/content/64 46b81f-a1b4-492f-b335-62f0efe11e7c.

60. Andrew Ross Sorkin et al., "BlackRock Forges a New Bond with Big Oil," *New York Times,* July 18, 2023, https://www.nytimes.com/2023/07/18/business /dealbook/blackrock-aramco-nasser-board.html.

61. Bivona and Taricco to Fink, November 10, 2022.

62. Tim McDonnell, "New York City's Climate-Conscious Pension Funds Put BlackRock on Notice," Semafor, January 27, 2023, https://www.semafor.com/artic le/01/27/2023/new-york-citys-climate-conscious-pension-funds-put-blackrock-on -notice.

63. Ropes & Gray, "Navigating State Regulation of ESG."

64. Sam Meredith, "World's Biggest Investment Fund Says Firms Mismanaging Climate Risk Could Face Exclusion from Next Year," CNBC, May 31, 2023, https:// www.cnbc.com/2023/05/31/norways-oil-fund-says-firms-mismanaging-climate -could-face-exclusion.html.

65. Dieter Holger, "At Least 10,000 Foreign Companies to Be Hit by EU Sustainability Rules," *Wall Street Journal,* April 5, 2023, https://www.wsj.com/articles /at-least-10-000-foreign-companies-to-be-hit-by-eu-sustainability-rules-307a1406.

66. Carl C. Icahn, "Carl C. Icahn Files Definitive Proxy Statement and Issues Open Letter to Shareholders of McDonald's Corporation," April 21, 2022, https:// carlicahn.com/carl-c-icahn-files-definitive-proxy-statement-and-issues-open -letter-to-shareholders-of-mcdonalds-corporation/.

67. Office of Governor Gavin Newsom, "Governor Newsom: California Pulls Back Renewal of Walgreens Contract," March 8, 2023, https://www.gov.ca.gov/20 23/03/08/governor-newsom-california-pulls-back-renewal-of-walgreens-contract/.

5. Doers, Talkers, Fence-Sitters, and Straddlers

1. Adelaide Martins, Delfina Gomes, and Manuel Castelo Branco, "Managing Corporate Social and Environmental Disclosure: An Accountability vs. Impression Management Framework," *Sustainability* 13, no. 1 (2020): 296, https://doi.org/10 .3390/su13010296.

2. Singleton, "Navigating ESG in the New Congress," 11.

3. Shaul Gayle, Tayler J. James, and Carlin Nelson, "2022 State of the Pledge: Revisiting Tech Organizations' Statements to Create a More Equitable Society for Black Americans through Diversity Recruitment Efforts and Investments," The Plug, 2022, https://static1.squarespace.com/static/5d9550357bc7f16776f6baed/t/ 6297ed89d6d6b576260f0280/1654123925483/state-of-the-pledge-case-study.pdf.

4. Armstrong, Edwards, and Pinder, "Corporate Commitments to Racial Justice," 4.

5. Satya Nadella, "Change in Ourselves Helps Drive Change in the World," Microsoft Corporate Blogs, June 5, 2020, https://blogs.microsoft.com/blog/2020/06 /05/change-in-ourselves-helps-drive-change-in-the-world/.

6. Satya Nadella, "Addressing Racial Injustice," Microsoft Corporate Blogs, June 23, 2020, https://blogs.microsoft.com/blog/2020/06/23/addressing-racial-injustice/.

7. Microsoft, *Microsoft Global Diversity & Inclusion Report 2022,* 2022, 17, https:// www.microsoft.com/en-us/diversity/inside-microsoft/annual-report.

8. Microsoft, "Microsoft's Racial Equity Initiative" (fact sheet), June 16, 2022, 2, https://query.prod.cms.rt.microsoft.com/cms/api/am/binary/RE4ZUFF.

9. Hugh Son, "'Appalled'—Here's What Wall Street CEOs Are Saying about the Killing of George Floyd and Protests Rocking US Cities," CNBC, June 1, 2020, https://www.cnbc.com/2020/06/01/wall-street-ceos-speak-out-about-george-floyd-and-protests-rocking-us-cities.html.

10. Wells Fargo, "Wells Fargo CEO: 'A Watershed Moment,'" June 19, 2020. See a reference to Charlie Scharf's pledge in a letter sent via email from Craig Leen, US Department of Labor Office of Federal Compliance Programs, to Michelle Duncan, Esq., and Jackson Lewis, PC, ERCA Counsel for Wells Fargo, September 29, 2020. Uploaded by Khristopher J. Brooks, Scribd, October 9, 2020, https://www.scribd.com/document/479372154/Wells-Fargo-Letter.

11. Jessica DiNapoli and Anirban Sen, "Wells Fargo CEO Sorry for 'Insensitive Comment' on Diversity," Reuters, September 23, 2020, https://www.reuters.com/article/idUSKCN26E07O.

12. Isabella Jibilian, "Elizabeth Warren, AOC Blast Wells Fargo CEO for Blaming 'Very Limited Pool of Black Talent' for the Bank's Trouble Hitting Its Diversity-Hiring Goals," *Business Insider*, September 23, 2020, https://www.businessinsider.com/aoc-sherrod-brown-criticize-wells-fargo-ceo-scharf-black-talent-2020-9.

13. Emily Flitter, "At Wells Fargo, a Quest to Increase Diversity Leads to Fake Job Interviews," *New York Times*, May 19, 2022, https://www.nytimes.com/2022/05/19/business/wells-fargo-fake-interviews.html.

14. Consumer Financial Protection Bureau, "Consumer Financial Protection Bureau Fines Wells Fargo $100 Million for Widespread Illegal Practice of Secretly Opening Unauthorized Accounts," September 8, 2016, https://www.consumerfinance.gov/about-us/newsroom/consumer-financial-protection-bureau-fines-wells-fargo-100-million-widespread-illegal-practice-secretly-opening-unauthorized-accounts/.

15. US Department of Justice, Office of Public Affairs, "Wells Fargo Agrees to Pay $3 Billion to Resolve Criminal and Civil Investigations into Sales Practices Involving the Opening of Millions of Accounts without Customer Authorization," February 21, 2020, https://www.justice.gov/opa/pr/wells-fargo-agrees-pay-3-billion-resolve-criminal-and-civil-investigations-sales-practices.

16. Wells Fargo, "Wells Fargo Response to New York Times Article," June 9, 2022, https://newsroom.wf.com/English/news-releases/news-release-details/2022/Wells-Fargo-response-to-New-York-Times-article/default.aspx.

17. Wells Fargo, "2022 Diversity, Equity, and Inclusion Report: Colleagues, Customers, Communities," July 2022, 7, https://www08.wellsfargomedia.com/assets/pdf/about/corporate/2022-diversity-equity-inclusion-report.pdf.

18. JPMorgan Chase, "JPMorgan Chase Commits $30 Billion to Advance Racial Equity," October 8, 2020, https://www.jpmorganchase.com/news-stories/jpmc-commits-30-billion-to-advance-racial-equity.

19. Emily Flitter, "This Is What Racism Sounds Like in the Banking Industry," *New York Times*, December 11, 2019, https://www.nytimes.com/2019/12/11/business/jpmorgan-banking-racism.html; and Sherrod Brown et al. letter to James

Dimon, December 19, 2019, https://www.banking.senate.gov/imo/media/doc/20
19.12.19%20-%20Letter%20to%20JPMC.pdf.

20. Hugh Son, "Jamie Dimon Says He's 'Disgusted by Racism' and Progress Is
Needed at JP Morgan after Report," CNBC, December 13, 2019, https://www.cnbc
.com/2019/12/13/jamie-dimon-says-hes-disgusted-by-racism-and-progress-is-need
ed-at-jp-morgan-after-report.html.

21. Jamie Dimon, "Chairman & CEO Letter to Shareholders: JPMorgan Chase
& Co. Annual Report 2021," April 4, 2022, https://reports.jpmorganchase.com/in
vestor-relations/2021/ar-ceo-letters.htm.

22. Emily Flitter, "Where $30 Billion to Fix Systemic Racism Actually Goes," *New
York Times*, October 21, 2022, https://www.nytimes.com/2022/10/21/business/jp
-morgan-racial-equity-pledge.html.

23. Ciara Linnane, "JPMorgan's $30 Billion Racial-Equity Commitment Was the
Biggest of Any U.S. Company. How Much Progress Has It Made?," MarketWatch,
May 25, 2022, updated May 31, 2022, https://www.marketwatch.com/story/jpmorg
ans-30-billion-racial-equity-commitment-was-the-biggest-of-any-u-s-company-how
-much-progress-has-it-made-11653476701.

24. Ban the Box, "About: The Ban the Box Campaign," accessed February 1,
2023, http://bantheboxcampaign.org/about/.

25. Jamie Dimon, "If You Paid Your Debt to Society, You Should Be Allowed to
Work," *New York Times*, August 4, 2021, https://www.nytimes.com/2021/08/04/op
inion/clean-slate-incarceration-work.html.

26. Florida CS/CS/HB 155, "Parental Rights in Education."

27. Madeleine Roberts, "New CDC Data Shows LGBTQ Youth Are More Likely
to Be Bullied Than Straight Cisgender Youth," Human Rights Campaign, August
26, 2020, https://www.hrc.org/news/new-cdc-data-shows-lgbtq-youth-are-more
-likely-to-be-bullied-than-straight-cisgender-youth.

28. Bob Iger and Christine McCarthy, "Walt Disney Company, Q2 FY23 Earnings Conference Call," moderated by Alexia Quadrani, May 10, 2023, 18, https://
thewaltdisneycompany.com/app/uploads/2023/05/q2-fy23-earnings-transcript.pdf.

29. While it is impossible to know precisely how many Disney employees identify as LGBTQ+, Disney had 166,000 employees in the United States in 2022 (see
Walt Disney Company, *Fiscal Year 2022 Annual Financial Report*, 2023, 2, https://
thewaltdisneycompany.com/app/uploads/2023/02/2022-Annual-Report.pdf). A
Pew Research Center poll found that 7 percent of Americans identify as lesbian, gay,
or bisexual, and 1.6 percent identify as transgender or nonbinary (see Anna Brown,
"5 Key Findings about LGBTQ+ Americans," Pew Research Center, June 23, 2023,
https://www.pewresearch.org/short-reads/2023/06/23/5-key-findings-about-lgb
tq-americans/). A Gallup survey put LGBT identification at 7.2 percent two years
in a row (see Jeffrey M. Jones, "U.S. LGBT Identification Steady at 7.2%," Gallup,
February 22, 2023, https://news.gallup.com/poll/470708/lgbt-identification-steady
.aspx). Even if members of Disney's US workforce are only half as likely to identify
as LGBTQ+ as Gallup's nationally representative surveys suggest, that totals nearly
6,000 employees.

30. Brian Moynihan, interview by David Westin, "Bank of America CEO Says

North Carolina Bathroom Law Is Bad for Business," Bloomberg Television, December 22, 2016, https://www.youtube.com/watch?v=eI-EVAoABos.

31. David Gelles, "Corporations, Vocal about Racial Justice, Go Quiet on Voting Rights," *New York Times*, March 29, 2021, updated April 5, 2021, https://www.nytimes.com/2021/03/29/business/corporate-america-voting-rights.html.

32. Delta, "Delta Ends NRA Discount"; and Uria, "Georgia Lawmakers Pass Tax Bill."

33. Chenault et al., "Memo to Corporate America"; and Shepardson and Kumar, "Delta, Coca-Cola Blast."

34. Unnikrishnan, "Delta Nearly Loses."

35. Mehta, " 'It Was Not an Issue.' "

36. Robert Iger (@RobertIger), "I'm with the President on this! If passed, this bill will put vulnerable, young LGBTQ people in jeopardy," Twitter, February 24, 2022, 11:21 p.m., https://twitter.com/RobertIger/status/1497064238145171458.

37. *Good Morning America* (@GMA), "NEW: Disney responds to protests and calls for action surrounding Florida's 'Don't Say Gay' Bill, saying in part, 'The biggest impact we can have in creating a more inclusive world is through the inspiring content we produce,' " Twitter, March 3, 2022, 9:17 p.m., https://twitter.com/GMA/status/1499569682952732672.

38. Scott Maxwell, "Florida's Anti-Gay Crusade Is Funded by the Disneys of the World," *Orlando Sentinel*, February 25, 2022, https://www.orlandosentinel.com/opinion/scott-maxwell-commentary/os-prem-op-florida-business-disney-dont-say-gay-scott-maxwell-20220225-b7pxbrc4pfdmxbm2ypo5bpw23e-story.html.

39. Gary Fineout, "Disney Gave $190K to Support Florida Republicans as Lawmakers Met," *Politico*, April 11, 2022, https://www.politico.com/news/2022/04/11/disney-donation-florida-republicans-00024417.

40. Dominic Patten, "Disney Boss Bob Chapek Says Company Won't Slam Florida's 'Don't Say Gay' Bill Directly, but Still Committed to Inclusion," Deadline, March 7, 2022, https://deadline.com/2022/03/disney-dont-say-gay-bill-florida-bob-chapek-lgbtq-ron-desantis-1234972655/.

41. Bob Chapek, speaker, report of Walt Disney Company, "2022 Annual Meeting of Shareholders," March 9, 2022, 32–33, https://thewaltdisneycompany.com/app/uploads/2022/03/2022-ASM-transcript.pdf.

42. Ryan Lattanzio, "Disney CEO Bob Chapek Apologizes to LGBTQ Employees, Pauses Political Donations in Florida," IndieWire, March 11, 2022, https://www.indiewire.com/2022/03/disney-ceo-bob-chapek-apologizes-lgbtq-employees-donations-1234707062/.

43. Brooks Barnes, "Disney Employees Walk out amid Furor over Florida Legislation," *New York Times*, March 22, 2022, https://www.nytimes.com/2022/03/22/business/media/disney-florida-employee-protests.html.

44. Florida House of Representatives, Florida SB 4-C, "Independent Special Districts," 2022, https://www.myfloridahouse.gov/Sections/Bills/billsdetail.aspx?BillId=76721.

45. S. V. Dáte, "DeSantis about to Defuse $1.2 Billion Tax Bomb He Activated a Year Ago to Punish Disney," *HuffPost*, February 21, 2023, updated February 23,

2023, https://www.huffpost.com/entry/florida-gop-governor-ron-desantis-disney -tax-bomb_n_63f541f7e4b0e2590d40098e.

46. Staff of Ron DeSantis, "Governor Ron DeSantis Signs Legislation Ending the Corporate Kingdom of Walt Disney World," February 27, 2023, https://www.flg ov.com/2023/02/27/governor-ron-desantis-signs-legislation-ending-the-corporate -kingdom-of-walt-disney-world/.

47. Skyler Swisher, "DeSantis' Reedy Creek Board Says Disney Stripped Its Power," *Orlando Sentinel*, March 29, 2023, https://www.orlandosentinel.com/news /os-ne-disney-new-reedy-creek-board-powerless-20230329-qalagcs4wjfe3iwkp zjsz2v4qm-story.html. See also "Disney Agreements" ("Declaration of Restrictive Covenants"), uploaded by Skyler Swisher, Scribd, February 8, 2023, https://www .scribd.com/document/634713441/Disney-agreements#.

48. Brooks Barnes, "Disney's Top Communications Executive Is out after Less Than Four Months," *New York Times*, April 29, 2022, https://www.nytimes.com/20 22/04/29/business/geoff-morrell-disney-out.html.

49. Matthew Belloni, "Meet Disney's New Oily Public Face," *Puck*, December 9, 2021, https://puck.news/meet-disneys-oily-new-public-face/.

50. Jessica Chasmar and Kelly Laco, "DeSantis Slams 'Woke' Disney after CEO Condemns Parents' Rights Bill," Fox News, March 10, 2022, https://www.foxnews .com/politics/desantis-woke-disney-ceo-parents-rights-bill.

51. Walt Disney Company, "Disney Board Extends Bob Chapek's Contract as CEO for Three Years," June 28, 2022, https://thewaltdisneycompany.com/disney -board-extends-bob-chapeks-contract-as-ceo-for-three-years/.

52. Brooks Barnes, "Disney Brings Back Bob Iger after Ousting Chapek as C.E.O.," *New York Times*, November 20, 2022, https://www.nytimes.com/2022/11 /20/business/disney-robert-iger.html.

53. *Walt Disney Parks and Resorts U.S., Inc., v. Ronald DeSantis et al.*, No. 4:23-cv-00163-MW-MAF, US District Court, Northern District, Florida, 2023, https://s3.documentcloud.org/documents/23789600/file-stamped-disney-com plaint1.pdf.

54. Iger and McCarthy, "Disney, Q2 FY23 Earnings Conference Call," 18.

55. Andrew Ross Sorkin et al., "Disney Inflicts a Blow to DeSantis ahead of His Presidential Run," *New York Times*, May 19, 2023, https://www.nytimes.com/2023 /05/19/business/dealbook/disney-desantis-presidential-campaign.html.

56. Florida House of Representatives, Florida CS/CS/HB 1069, "Education," 2023, https://www.flsenate.gov/Session/Bill/2023/1069/BillText/er/PDF.

57. Brooks Barnes, "With DeSantis on the Stump, Disney Sees a Long Campaign Ahead," *New York Times*, July 3, 2023, https://www.nytimes.com/2023/07/03/busi ness/disney-ron-desantis-criticism.html.

58. Axios Harris Poll, "The Axios Harris Poll 100 Reputation Rankings," *Axios*, March 6, 2019, https://www.axios.com/2019/03/06/axios-harris-poll-corporate -reputations; and Axios Harris Poll, "2023 Axios Harris Poll."

59. Axios Harris Poll, "The 2020 Axios Harris Poll 100 Reputation Rankings," *Axios*, July 30, 2020, https://www.axios.com/2020/07/30/axios-harris-poll-corpora te-reputations-2020; Axios Harris Poll, "The 2021 Axios Harris Poll 100 Reputation

Rankings," *Axios*, May 13, 2021, https://www.axios.com/2021/05/13/the-2021-axios-harris-poll-100-reputation-rankings; and Axios Harris Poll, "2022 Axios Harris Poll."

60. Global Strategy Group, "Shifting Politics of Doing Good," 7.

61. Iger and McCarthy, "Disney Q2 FY23 Earnings Conference Call," 12.

62. Yale School of Management, "Data from Prof. Jeffrey Sonnenfeld Propels Corporate Action on Russia," March 11, 2022, https://som.yale.edu/story/2022/data-prof-jeffrey-sonnenfeld-propels-corporate-action-russia.

63. Yale School of Management, Yale CELI List of Companies Leaving and Staying in Russia, "About," 2022, https://www.yalerussianbusinessretreat.com/about.

64. Jeffrey Sonnenberg, "Let's Say Gay, the US Bans Russian Oil, and Guest Jeffrey Sonnenfeld," interview by Kara Swisher and Scott Galloway, *Pivot*, Vox Media, episode 284, March 11, 2022, 35:44–36:02.

65. Brian Chesky (@bchesky), "Airbnb is suspending all operations in Russia and Belarus," Twitter, March 3, 2022, 11:02 p.m., https://twitter.com/bchesky/status/1499596215389863939?s=20&t=h4vjJg8dvo-naLDiqa3rFQ.

66. Brian Chesky, "'Heartbreaking.' Airbnb CEO Promises Free Housing for Ukraine's Refugees," interview by Matt Egan, CNN Business, March 2, 2022, 0:46–0:52, https://www.cnn.com/videos/business/2022/03/02/brian-chesky-airbnb-ukraine-refugees-gr-orig.cnn.

67. Shell plc, "Shell Announces Intent to Withdraw from Russian Oil and Gas," March 8, 2022, https://shell.gcs-web.com/news-releases/news-release-details/shell-announces-intent-withdraw-russian-oil-and-gas.

68. Jeffrey Sonnenfeld et al., "It Pays for Companies to Leave Russia," last revised May 31, 2022, http://dx.doi.org/10.2139/ssrn.4112885.

69. BP, "bp to Exit Rosneft Shareholding," February 27, 2022, https://www.bp.com/en/global/corporate/news-and-insights/press-releases/bp-to-exit-rosneft-shareholding.html.

70. BP, "bp's Position in Russia," December 9, 2022, https://www.bp.com/en/global/corporate/news-and-insights/press-releases/bps-position-in-russia.html.

71. Brianne McGonigle Leyh and Marie Elske Gispen, "Access to Medicines in Times of Conflict: Overlapping Compliance and Accountability Frameworks for Syria," *Health and Human Rights* 20, no. 1 (2018): 237, https://www.ncbi.nlm.nih.gov/pmc/articles/PMC6039728/.

72. Pfizer, "Pfizer Updates Company Position in Russia," March 14, 2022, https://www.pfizer.com/news/press-release/press-release-detail/pfizer-updates-company-position-russia.

73. Sally Susman, *Breaking Through: Communicating to Open Minds, Move Hearts, and Change the World* (Boston: Harvard Business Review Press, 2022), 10.

74. Brian McCollum, "Kid Rock: Confederate Flag Was Dropped Years before Protest," *Detroit Free Press*, July 16, 2015, https://www.freep.com/story/entertainment/music/2015/07/16/kid-rock-flown-confederate-flag-five-years/30226159/; and Businedu, "Kid Rock Responds to Bud Light's Dylan Mulvaney Campaign #twogenders," April 4, 2023, https://youtube.com/shorts/qDE3L4c41Ds?feature=share.

75. Matt Walsh (@MattWalshBlog), Twitter, April 5, 2023, 5:04 p.m., https://twitter.com/MattWalshBlog/status/1643721182280142851.

76. Saabira Chaudhuri, "Bud Brewer AB InBev Loses Its Luster in the U.S.," *Wall Street Journal*, July 28, 2022, https://www.wsj.com/articles/bud-brewer-ab-in bev-loses-its-luster-in-the-u-s-11659004233; and Distilled Spirits Council, "Distilled Spirits Council Annual Economic Briefing: Reaching Historic Milestone, U.S. Spir-its Revenues Take Share Lead of Total U.S. Beverage Alcohol Market in 2022," February 9, 2023, https://www.distilledspirits.org/news/distilled-spirits-council-an nual-economic-briefing-reaching-historic-milestone-u-s-spirits-revenues-take -share-lead-of-total-u-s-beverage-alcohol-market-in-2022/.

77. Jennifer Maloney, "Beer Drinkers Cut Back as Bud Brewer AB InBev Raises Prices," *Wall Street Journal*, March 2, 2023, https://www.wsj.com/articles/beer -drinkers-cut-back-as-bud-brewer-ab-inbev-raises-prices-e9ed8a24.

78. Bondi, Burbano, and Dell'Acqua. "When to Talk Politics," 33.

79. Kim Parker, Juliana Menasce Horowitz, and Anna Brown, "Americans' Com-plex Views on Gender Identity and Transgender Issues," Pew Research Center, June 28, 2022, https://www.pewresearch.org/social-trends/2022/06/28/americans-com plex-views-on-gender-identity-and-transgender-issues/.

80. Another explanation is that boycotts provide an opportunity for consumers to take part in collective action, while buycotts tend to be individual endorsements. See Marc Jungblut and Marius Johnen, "When Brands (Don't) Take My Stance: The Ambiguous Effectiveness of Political Brand Communication," *Communication Research* 49, no. 8 (2022): 1092–117.

81. Anheuser-Busch (@AnheuserBusch), "Our Responsibility to America," Twitter, April 14, 2023, 3:32 p.m., https://twitter.com/AnheuserBusch/status/1646 959620437561356. The full text of the post is also on the Anheuser-Busch website: https://www.anheuser-busch.com/newsroom/our-responsibility-to-america.

82. Target, "Target Statement on 2023 Pride Collection," May 24, 2023, https://corporate.target.com/press/releases/2023/05/Target-Statement-on-2023-Pride -Collection; and Dominick Reuter, "Target CEO Defends the Decision to Remove Pride Displays and Pledges to Support the LGBTQ Community. Read His Letter to Employees," *Insider*, May 25, 2023, https://www.businessinsider.com/target-ceo -brian-cornell-defends-decision-remove-pride-displays-email-2023-5.

83. Jennifer Maloney, "Bud Light Loses Title as Top-Selling U.S. Beer," *Wall Street Journal*, June 14, 2023, https://www.wsj.com/articles/bud-light-modelo-best -selling-beer-6a4d6b27.

84. Brendan Whitworth, "Anheuser-Busch Announces Support for Frontline Employees and Wholesaler Partners," Anheuser-Busch, June 15, 2023, https://www .anheuser-busch.com/newsroom/support-for-frontline-employees-and-wholesaler -partners; and Jordan Valinsky, "Anheuser-Busch Hopes Its New Ads Will Change the Conversation," CNN, June 28, 2023, https://www.cnn.com/2023/06/28/busi ness/anheuser-busch-employee-ad-campaign/index.html.

85. "Anheuser-Busch InBev/NV (BUD) Q2 2023 Earnings Call Transcript," Mot-ley Fool, August 3, 2023, https://www.fool.com/earnings/call-transcripts/2023/08 /03/anheuser-busch-inbevnv-bud-q2-2023-earnings-call-t/.

86. John Yoon, "Transgender Influencer Speaks Out after Backlash against Bud Light," *New York Times*, June 29, 2023, https://www.nytimes.com/2023/06/29/bus iness/bud-light-dylan-mulvaney.html.

6. Listen First

1. DiNapoli and Sen, "Wells Fargo CEO Sorry."

2. Edelman, *Business and Racial Justice*, 18.

3. I am grateful to Cameron Anderson for his insights about this.

4. Adam D. Galinsky et al., "Power and Perspectives Not Taken," *Psychological Science* 17, no. 12 (2006): 1072; and Steven L. Blader, Aiwa Shirako, and Ya-Ru Chen, "Looking Out from the Top," *Personality and Social Psychology Bulletin* 42, no. 6 (2016): 732.

5. Leigh Plunkett Tost, Francesca Gino, and Richard P. Larrick, "Power, Competitiveness, and Advice Taking: Why the Powerful Don't Listen," *Organizational Behavior and Human Decision Processes* 117, no. 1 (2012): 33.

6. Sadun et al., "C-Suite Skills That Matter Most," 148.

7. Mitchell, Agle, and Wood, "Toward a Theory of Stakeholder Identification," 854.

8. Bivona and Taricco to Fink, November 10, 2022.

9. Dr. Paul Y. Song, in discussion with author, June 24, 2022.

10. Recall the post by Walsh (@MattWalshBlog, Twitter, April 5, 2023, 5:04 p.m.), for example.

11. Ed Hoffman, Matthew Kohut, and Larry Prusak, *The Smart Mission: NASA's Lessons for Managing Knowledge, People, and Projects* (Cambridge: MIT Press, 2022), 69; and Scott Galloway, "The Crypto Meltdown—with David Yermack," Vox Media, Prof G, episode 172, June 7, 2022, 9:54–10:02.

12. Edelman, *Trust in the Workplace*, 16.

13. American Airlines, "American Airlines Statement on Texas Voting Legislation," April 1, 2021, https://news.aa.com/news/news-details/2021/American-Air lines-Statement-on-Texas-Voting-Legislation-CORP-OTH-04/default.aspx.

14. Swisher, "American Airlines C.E.O."

15. Mark Tercek, in discussion with the author, August 21, 2021.

16. Cynthia Foronda et al., "Cultural Humility: A Concept Analysis," *Journal of Transcultural Nursing* 27, no. 3 (2016): 216.

17. Priscilla H. Douglas, "Affinity Groups: Catalyst for Inclusive Organizations," *Employment Relations Today* 34, no. 4 (2008): 12; and Theresa M. Welbourne, Skylar Rolf, and Steven Schlachter, "The Case for Employee Resource Groups: A Review and Social Identity Theory-Based Research Agenda," *Personnel Review* 46, no. 1 (2017): 1828.

18. Welbourne et al., 1818.

19. Rodriguez discussion with the author.

20. Eleanor Lacey, in discussion with the author, August 7, 2022.

21. Edelman, *Business and Racial Justice*, 23.

22. Maiman discussion with the author.

23. David Gelles, "Long before Beth Ford Became Land O' Lakes C.E.O., She Cleaned Toilets," *New York Times*, May 30, 2021, https://www.nytimes.com/2021/05/29/business/beth-ford-land-o-lakes-corner-office.html.

24. Maiman discussion with the author.

25. Rodriguez discussion with the author.

7. Lived Experience Matters

1. Lucas Grindley, "Apple's Newest Product: Gay iCon?," *The Advocate*, October 19, 2011, https://www.advocate.com/business/2011/10/19/apples-newest-product-gay-icon.

2. Tim Cook, "Tim Cook Speaks Up," Bloomberg, October 30, 2014, https://www.bloomberg.com/news/articles/2014-10-30/tim-cook-speaks-up.

3. Benjamin Snyder, "Apple's CEO Becomes the Fortune 500's Only Openly Gay CEO. Here Are 11 Other Workplace Stats," *Fortune*, October 30, 2014, https://fortune.com/2014/10/30/apples-ceo-becomes-the-fortune-500s-only-openly-gay-ceo-here-are-11-more-workplace-stats/.

4. Jeb Su, "CNBC Host Accidentally Outs Apple CEO Tim Cook as Gay," *Forbes*, June 27, 2014, https://www.forbes.com/sites/jeanbaptiste/2014/06/27/cnbc-host-accidentally-outs-apple-ceo-tim-cook-as-gay-video/?sh=783f2a2c241b.

5. Tim Carmody, "From Rumor to Out: Tim Cook Reminds Us that 'Unpublishable' Facts Don't Live in a Vacuum Online," *Nieman Lab*, October 31, 2014, https://www.niemanlab.org/2014/10/from-rumor-to-out-tim-cook-reminds-us-that-unpublishable-facts-dont-live-in-an-vacuum-online/.

6. Jeff Goodell, "Steve Jobs in 1994: The Rolling Stone Interview," *Rolling Stone*, January 17, 2011, https://www.rollingstone.com/culture/culture-news/steve-jobs-in-1994-the-rolling-stone-interview-231132/.

7. Arjun Kharpal, "Apple's Tim Cook on Trump Immigration Ban: Steve Jobs Was the Son of an Immigrant," CNBC, February 9, 2017, https://www.cnbc.com/2017/02/09/apple-tim-cook-trump-immigration-ban-steve-jobs-son-of-an-immigrant.html.

8. Saheli Roy Choudhury, "Microsoft's Nadella: Trump Administration Policy Separating Children from Families Is 'Abhorrent,'" CNBC, June 20, 2018, https://www.cnbc.com/2018/06/20/microsoft-ceo-satya-nadella-on-trump-administration-immigrant-policy.html.

9. Brad Smith, "The Country Needs to Get Immigration Right," Microsoft on the Issues (blog), June 19, 2018, https://blogs.microsoft.com/on-the-issues/2018/06/19/the-country-needs-to-get-immigration-right/.

10. David Gelles, "Corner Office: The CEO of UPS on Voting Rights and Vaccine Delivery," *New York Times*, June 17, 2021, https://www.nytimes.com/2021/06/17/business/carole-tome-ups-corner-office.html.

11. Macaela MacKenzie, "Why CEOs Need to Talk about Mental Health," *Forbes*, May 15, 2018, https://www.forbes.com/sites/macaelamackenzie/2018/05/15/mental-health-awareness-month-why-ceos-need-to-talk-about-mental-health/?sh=361d245e53c2.

12. Matthew Cooper, "I'm Stepping Down as CEO due to My Mental Health— and I Want to Talk about It," *Quartz at Work*, December 18, 2020, https://qz.com /work/1947585/earnups-matthew-cooper-im-leaving-as-ceo-due-to-mental-health.

13. Lynch interview by King.

14. Amy Gilliland, interview by Geoff Bennett, *NewsHour*, PBS, October 28, 2022, 1:50–2:05, https://twitter.com/NewsHour/status/1578864723118161920.

15. Tugend, "For CEOs, Communication."

16. Thasunda Brown Duckett, "It's O.K. Not to Be O.K. Right Now," LinkedIn, June 8, 2020, https://www.linkedin.com/pulse/its-ok-right-now-thasunda-brown -duckett/.

17. Nick Corasaniti and Reid J. Epstein, "Georgia G.O.P. Fires Opening Shot in Fight to Limit Voting," *New York Times*, April 2, 2021, https://www.nytimes.com/20 21/03/26/us/politics/voting-rights-laws-georgia.html.

18. Chauncey Alcorn, "Black Fortune 500 Executives Want Companies to Fight Republican Voting Restrictions," CNN Business, March 31, 2021, https://www.cnn .com/2021/03/31/business/black-executives-voter-suppression/index.html.

19. Sorkin and Gelles, "Black Executives Call."

20. Chenault et al., "Memo to Corporate America."

21. David Gelles, "Delta and Coca-Cola Reverse Course on Georgia Voting Law, Stating 'Crystal Clear' Opposition," *New York Times*, March 31, 2021, https://www.ny times.com/2021/03/31/business/delta-coca-cola-georgia-voting-law.html.

22. Zoe Christen Jones and Grace Segers, "MLB Moves All-Star Game out of At- lanta in Response to Georgia's New Voting Law," CBS News, April 4, 2021, https:// www.cbsnews.com/news/georgia-voting-law-mlb-all-star-game-moved-out-atlanta /#:~:text=MLB%20reportedly%20giving%20All-Star%20game%20to%20Denver%20after%20say %20is%20designed%20to%20disenfranchise%20voters%20of%20color.

23. MacKenzie, "Why CEOs Need to Talk."

24. Chenault et al., "Memo to Corporate America."

8. Values Matter

1. Kiku Adatto, "Saving for Democracy: Thrift, Sacrifice, and the World War II Bond Campaigns," in *Thrift and Thriving in America: Capitalism and Moral Order from the Puritans to the Present*, eds. Joshua Yates and James Davison Hunter, ch. 16 (New York: Oxford University Press, 2011).

2. Melanie Warner, "OPENERS: SUITS; Cup of Coffee, Grain of Salt," *New York Times*, December 26, 2004, https://www.nytimes.com/2004/12/26/business /openers-suits-cup-of-coffee-grain-of-salt.html.

3. Thomas J. Peters and Robert H. Waterman Jr., *In Search of Excellence: Lessons from America's Best-Run Companies* (New York: Warner Books, 1982), 9; and Free- man, *Strategic Management*, 86.

4. Dana Minbaeva, Larissa Rabbiosi, and Günter K. Stahl, "Not Walking the Talk? How Host Country Cultural Orientations May Buffer the Damage of Corpo- rate Values' Misalignment in Multinational Corporations," *Journal of World Business* 53, no. 6 (2018): 880–95.

5. Gelles, "CEO of UPS on Voting Rights."

6. Swisher, "American Airlines C.E.O."

7. Amy L. Kristof-Brown, Ryan D. Zimmerman, and Erin C. Johnson, "Consequences of Individuals' Fit at Work: A Meta-Analysis of Person–Job, Person–Organization, Person–Group, and Person–Supervisor Fit," *Personnel Psychology* 58, no. 2 (2005): 326.

8. Jerry Allison, "Values Statements," *International Journal of Organizational Analysis* 27, no. 3 (2019): 666–89.

9. Maiman discussion with the author.

10. Edelman, *Trust in the Workplace*, 13.

11. Burbano, "Demotivating Effects."

12. Edelman, *Trust in the Workplace*, 12.

13. Song discussion with the author.

14. David Gelles, "Corner Office: An Optimist at the Helm of IBM," *New York Times*, May 13, 2022, https://www.nytimes.com/2022/05/13/business/arvind-krishna-ibm-corner-office.html.

15. David Gelles, "Corner Office: The C.E.O. Taking On the Gun Lobby," *New York Times*, October 25, 2019, https://www.nytimes.com/2019/10/25/business/ed-stack-dicks-sporting-goods-corner-office.html.

16. Edelman, *2023 Global Report*, 28.

17. Dick's Sporting Goods, Inc., "Q3 2018 Earnings Call," November 28, 2018, 5, https://s27.q4cdn.com/812551136/files/doc_financials/2018/q3/3q18-transcript.pdf.

18. Axios, "2022 Axios Harris Poll."

19. Thuermer, "Patagonia Dumps Jackson Hole."

20. Charles Duhigg, "What Google Learned from Its Quest to Build the Perfect Team," *New York Times Magazine*, February 25, 2016, https://www.nytimes.com/2016/02/28/magazine/what-google-learned-from-its-quest-to-build-the-perfect-team.html.

21. Nadella, "Change in Ourselves."

22. Tugend, "For CEOs, Communication."

23. Gulati, *Deep Purpose*, 110.

24. Alex Laskey, in discussion with the author, August 12, 2022.

25. Colleen Rowe, "Penguin Random House Is Committed to Protecting the Freedom to Read," Penguin Random House, June 27, 2023, https://penguinrandomhousesecondaryeducation.com/2023/06/27/freedom-to-read/.

26. Cook, "Legacy of Steve Jobs," 18:55–19:30.

27. Lynch interview by King.

28. Gelles, "Optimist at the Helm of IBM."

29. Richard Socarides, in discussion with the author, August 1, 2022.

9. Values Are Not Enough

1. Tercek discussion with the author.

2. Weihl, "ClimateVoices Featuring Paul Polman."

3. Axios Harris Poll 100 results in Hawkins, "By the Numbers."

4. Queenie Wong, "Former Pinterest Employees Say They Faced Racial Discrimination and Were Underpaid," CNET, June 15, 2023, https://www.cnet.com/culture/former-pinterest-employees-say-they-faced-racial-discrimination-and-were-underpaid/.

5. Ifeoma Ozoma (@IfeomaOzoma), "As a Black woman, seeing @Pinterest's middle of the night 'Black employees matter' statement made me scratch my head after I just fought for over a full year to be paid and leveled fairly . . . 2/," Twitter, June 15, 2020, 11:07 a.m., https://twitter.com/IfeomaOzoma/status/1272546222448885760.

6. Edelman, *Business and Racial Justice*, 25.

7. Rodriguez discussion with the author.

8. Gartner, Inc., "Gartner Identifies Three Dimensions That Define the New Employer-Employee Relationship," *Businesswire*, October 13, 2020, https://www.businesswire.com/news/home/20201013005956/en/Gartner-Identifies-Three-Dimensions-That-Define-The-New-Employer-Employee-Relationship.

9. Neffinger and Kohut, *Compelling People*, xv. See also Amy J. C. Cuddy, Matthew Kohut, and John Neffinger, "Connect, Then Lead," *Harvard Business Review* 91, nos. 7–8 (July–August 2013): 55–61.

10. Schulman, "PayPal Withdraws Plan."

11. BP, "bp to Exit Rosneft Shareholding."

12. Frazier, "Statement from Kenneth C. Frazier."

13. Ceres, "About Us," accessed March 31, 2023, https://www.ceres.org/about-us.

14. Ceres, "Ceres Investor Network on Climate Risk and Sustainability," accessed March 31, 2023, https://www.ceres.org/networks/ceres-investor-network.

15. Climate Action 100+, "About," accessed March 31, 2023, https://www.climateaction100.org/about/.

16. Letter from Arizona attorney general Mark Brnovich (and signed by eighteen other attorneys general) to Larry Fink, August 4, 2022, https://www.azag.gov/sites/default/files/2022-08/BlackRock%20Letter.pdf.

17. Letter from Rep. Dan Bishop et al. to Ceres CEO Mindy Lubber and CalPERS managing investment director for global equity Simiso Nzima, December 6, 2022, https://judiciary.house.gov/sites/evo-subsites/republicans-judiciary.house.gov/files/legacy_files/wp-content/uploads/2022/12/2022-12-06-HJC-GOP-to-Lubber-Nzima-re-ESG.pdf.

18. Bryan, "COP27: Mark Carney"; and James Dyke, Robert Watson, and Wolfgang Knorr, "Climate Scientists: Concept of Net Zero Is a Dangerous Trap," *The Conversation*, April 22, 2021, https://theconversation.com/climate-scientists-concept-of-net-zero-is-a-dangerous-trap-157368.

19. Gadinis and Havasy, "Quest for Legitimacy," 36.

20. Hambrick and Wowak, "CEO Sociopolitical Activism," 43–45.

21. CEO Action for Diversity & Inclusion, "Businesses Can ACT ON Making Change Happen," accessed March 17, 2023, https://www.ceoaction.com/actions/.

22. Long-Term Stock Exchange, "Listing Standards," accessed November 6, 2023, https://assets.website-files.com/6462417e8db99f8baa069524/6495ea2a874396d6201beob8_ListingStandard2023.pdf.

23. B Lab, "About Our Standards," accessed March 25, 2023, https://www.bco rporation.net/en-us/standards.

24. Gadinis and Havasy, "Quest for Legitimacy," 37–38.

25. Dieter Holter, "Companies Make EEOC Diversity Disclosures Public Amid Investor Pressure," *Wall Street Journal*, September 1, 2021, https://www.wsj.com/ar ticles/companies-make-eeoc-diversity-disclosures-public-amid-investor-pressure-11 630490400.

26. Amazon, "Notice of 2022 Annual Meeting of Shareholders & Proxy Statement," May 25, 2022, 49, https://s2.q4cdn.com/299287126/files/doc_financials /2022/ar/Amazon-2022-Proxy-Statement.pdf; and Citi, "Citi Will Conduct a Racial Equity Audit," October 22, 2021, https://www.citigroup.com/global/news/perspect ive/2021/citi-will-conduct-a-racial-equity-audit.

27. Lacey discussion with the author.

28. Noah J. Goldstein, Steve J. Martin, and Robert B. Cialdini, *Yes! 50 Scientifically Proven Ways to Be Persuasive* (New York: Free Press, 2008), 122.

10. Have a Process

1. Marc Benioff, "Marc Benioff's Toughest Conversation with Kara Swisher," interview by Kara Swisher, *On with Kara Swisher*, Vox Media, March 6, 2023, 24:41–25:25.

2. Kara Swisher, "Full Transcript: Facebook CEO Mark Zuckerberg on Recode Decode," *Vox*, July 18, 2018, https://www.vox.com/2018/7/18/17575158/mark-zucker berg-facebook-interview-full-transcript-kara-swisher.

3. Scott Galloway, "The Twitter Files, How to Make Good Business Decisions, and Guest Maria Ressa," interview by Kara Swisher, *Pivot*, Vox Media, episode 362, December 6, 2022, 31:40–33:37.

4. Steve Wyche, "Colin Kaepernick Explains Why He Sat during National Anthem," NFL.com, August 27, 2016, updated August 28, 2016, https://web.archive .org/web/20170820000932/http://www.nfl.com/news/story/0ap3000000691077/article/colin-kaepernick-explains-why-he-sat-during-national-anthem.

5. Kevin Draper, Julie Creswell, and Sapna Maheshwari, "Nike Returns to Familiar Strategy with Kaepernick Ad Campaign," *New York Times*, September 4, 2018, https://www.nytimes.com/2018/09/04/sports/nike-colin-kaepernick.html.

6. Galloway, "Twitter Files."

7. John D. Stoll, "When It Comes to Colin Kaepernick, the Flag and Nike, It's Just Business," *Wall Street Journal*, July 3, 2019, https://www.wsj.com/articles/when-it -comes-to-colin-kaepernick-the-flag-and-nike-its-just-business-11562161561.

8. Bondi, Burbano, and Dell'Acqua, "When to Talk Politics," 32.

9. Bondi, Burbano, and Dell'Acqua, 33–34.

10. Jūra Liaukonytė, Anna Tuchman, and Xinrong Zhu, "Frontiers: Spilling the Beans on Political Consumerism: Do Social Media Boycotts and Buycotts Translate to Real Sales Impact?," *Marketing Science* 42, no. 1 (2023): 11, https://doi.org/10.12 87/mksc.2022.1386.

11. Charlan Nemeth, Keith Brown, and John Rogers, "Devil's Advocate versus

Authentic Dissent: Stimulating Quantity and Quality," *European Journal of Social Psychology* 31, no. 6 (2001): 718.

12. Gary Klein, "Performing a Project Premortem," *Harvard Business Review* 85, no. 9 (2007): 18–19, https://hbr.org/2007/09/performing-a-project-premortem.

13. Tercek discussion with the author.

Afterword

1. Wilson, *New Rules of Corporate Conduct*, 129–30.

2. Heidrick & Struggles, "Board Monitor US 2023," 2023, 12–13, https://www.heidrick.com/-/media/heidrickcom/publications-and-reports/board-monitor-us-2023.pdf.

3. Wilson, *New Rules of Corporate Conduct*, 130.

4. For instance, as of this writing, the US Securities and Exchange Commission is expected to issue a final rule requiring standardized climate-related risk disclosures from publicly traded companies.

5. See, for instance, Dorothy S. Lund and Elizabeth Pollman, "The Corporate Governance Machine," *Columbia Law Review* 121 (2021): 2563.

6. Chip Cutter, "More Bosses Order Workers back to the Office as Job Market Shifts," *Wall Street Journal*, January 4, 2023, https://www.wsj.com/articles/more-bosses-order-workers-back-to-the-office-as-job-market-shifts-11672689665.

7. Marlatt, *What Consumers Expect from CEOs*, 6.

SELECTED BIBLIOGRAPHY

Bedendo, Mascia, and Linus Siming. "To Advocate or Not to Advocate: Determinants and Financial Consequences of CEO Activism." *British Journal of Management* 32, no. 4 (December 2021): 1062–81.

Benioff, Marc, and Monica Langley. *Trailblazer: The Power of Business as the Greatest Platform for Change.* New York: Currency, 2019.

Berle, Adolf A., and Gardiner C. Means. *The Modern Corporation and Private Property.* Rev. ed. New York: Harcourt, Brace & World, 1968.

Bondi, Tommaso, Vanessa Burbano, and Fabrizio Dell'Acqua. "When to Talk Politics in Business: Theory and Experimental Evidence of Stakeholder Responses to CEO Political Activism." Working paper. Cornell Tech and SC Johnson School of Management, Cornell University, New York, 2023.

Burbano, Vanessa C. "The Demotivating Effects of Communicating a Social-Political Stance: Field Experimental Evidence from an Online Labor Market Platform." *Management Science* 67, no. 2 (2021): 1004–25. https://doi.org/10.1287/mnsc.2019.3562.

Business Roundtable. "Statement on Corporate Responsibility." October 1981. https://ralphgomory.org/wp-content/uploads/2023/02/1981-Business-Roundtable-Statement-on-Corporate-Responsibility-11.pdf.

———. "Statement on the Purpose of a Corporation." August 19, 2019. https://www.businessroundtable.org/business-roundtable-redefines-the-purpose-of-a-corporation-to-promote-an-economy-that-serves-all-americans.

Chatterji, Aaron K., and Michael W. Toffel. "Assessing the Impact of CEO Activism." *Organization & Environment* 32, no. 2 (2019): 159–85.

———. "The New CEO Activists." *Harvard Business Review* 96, no. 1 (January–February 2018): 78–89. https://hbr.org/2018/01/the-new-ceo-activists.

Delmas, Magali A., and Vanessa Cuerel Burbano. "The Drivers of Greenwashing." *California Management Review* 54, no. 1 (2011): 64–87.

Denison, Daniel R., and Aneil K. Mishra. "Toward a Theory of Organizational Culture and Effectiveness." *Organization Science* 6, no. 2 (1995): 204–23.

Donaldson, Thomas, and Lee E. Preston. "The Stakeholder Theory of the Corporation: Concepts, Evidence, and Implications." *Academy of Management Review* 20, no. 1 (1995): 65–91. http://www.jstor.org/stable/258887.

Englander, Ernie, and Allen Kaufman. "The End of Managerial Ideology: From Corporate Social Responsibility to Corporate Social Indifference." *Enterprise and Society* 5, no 3 (2004): 404–50. doi:10.1093/es/khh058.

Flitter, Emily. *The White Wall: How Big Finance Bankrupts Black America.* New York: One Signal Publishers, 2022.

Fos, Vyacheslav, Elisabeth Kempf, and Margarita Tsoutsoura. "The Political Polarization of Corporate America." Working paper no. w30183. National Bureau of Economic Research, June 2022. http://dx.doi.org/10.2139/ssrn.3784969.

Freeman, R. Edward. *Strategic Management: A Stakeholder Approach.* Boston: Pitman, 1984.

Friedman, Milton. "A Friedman Doctrine—the Social Responsibility of Business Is to Increase Its Profits." *New York Times Magazine*, September 13, 1970. https://www.nytimes.com/1970/09/13/archives/a-friedman-doctrine-the-social-responsibility-of-business-is-to.html.

Giridharadas, Anand. *Winners Take All: The Elite Charade of Changing the World.* New York: Alfred A. Knopf, 2018.

Goodman, Peter S. *Davos Man: How the Billionaires Devoured the World.* New York: Custom House, 2022.

Gulati, Ranjay. *Deep Purpose: The Heart and Soul of High-Performance Companies.* New York: Harper Business, 2022.

Hambrick, Donald C., and Adam J. Wowak. "CEO Sociopolitical Activism: A Stakeholder Alignment Model." *Academy of Management Review* 46, no. 1 (January 2021): 33–59. https://doi.org/10.5465/amr.2018.0084.

Henderson, Rebecca. *Reimagining Capitalism in a World on Fire.* New York: Public Affairs, 2020.

Jensen, Michael C., and William H. Meckling. "Theory of the Firm: Managerial Behavior, Agency Costs and Ownership Structure." *Journal of Financial Economics* 3, no. 4 (1976): 305–60. http://dx.doi.org/10.2139/ssrn.94043.

Mackey, John, and Raj Sisodia. *Conscious Capitalism: Liberating the Heroic Spirit of Business.* Boston: Harvard Business School Publishing, 2014.

Mintzberg, Henry. *The Nature of Managerial Work.* New York: Harper & Row, 1973.

Mitchell, Ronald K., Bradley R. Agle, and Donna J. Wood. "Toward a Theory of Stakeholder Identification and Salience: Defining the Principle of Who and What Really Counts." *Academy of Management Review* 22, no. 4 (1997): 853–86.

Murray, Alan. *Tomorrow's Capitalist: My Search for the Soul of Business.* With Catherine Whitney. New York: Public Affairs, 2022.

Olkkonen, Laura, and Mette Morsing. "A Processual Model of CEO Activism: Activities, Frames, and Phases." *Business & Society* 62, no. 3 (2022): 646–94. https://doi.org/10.1177/00076503221110184.

Polman, Paul, and Andrew Winston. *Net Positive: How Courageous Companies Thrive by Giving More Than They Take.* Boston: Harvard Business Review Press, 2021.

Preston, Lee E., and James E. Post. *Private Management and Public Policy: The Principle of Public Responsibility.* Englewood Cliffs NJ: Prentice-Hall, 1975.

Ramaswamy, Vivek. *Woke, Inc.: Inside Corporate America's Social Justice Scam.* New York: Center Street, 2021.

Rumstadt, Franz, and Dominik K. Kanbach. "CEO Activism: What Do We Know? What Don't We Know? A Systematic Literature Review." *Society and Business Review* 17, no. 2 (2022): 307–30. https://doi.org/10.1108/SBR-10-2021-0194.

Schwab, Klaus. *Stakeholder Capitalism: A Global Economy that Works for Progress, People and Planet.* With Peter Vanham. Hoboken NJ: John Wiley & Sons, 2021.

Sonnenfeld, Jeffrey A. *Corporate Views of the Public Interest: Perceptions of the Forest Products Industry.* Boston: Auburn House, 1981.

Tedlow, Richard S. "The National Association of Manufacturers and Public Relations during the New Deal." *Business History Review* 50, no. 1 (1976): 25–45. http://www.jstor.org/stable/3113573.

Watson, Thomas J., Jr. *A Business and Its Beliefs: The Ideas That Helped Build IBM.* New York: McGraw-Hill, 1963.

Wilson, Ian. *The New Rules of Corporate Conduct: Rewriting the Corporate Charter.* Westport CT: Quorum Books, 2000.

Wowak, Adam J., John R. Busenbark, and Donald C. Hambrick. "How Do Employees React? When Their CEO Speaks Out? Intra- and Extra-Firm Implications of CEO Sociopolitical Activism." *Administrative Science Quarterly* 67, no. 2 (2022): 553–93.

Zammit-Lucia, Joseph. *The New Political Capitalism: How Businesses and Societies Can Thrive in a Deeply Politicized World.* London: Bloomsbury Business, 2022.

INDEX

158 INDEX

Frazier, Kenneth, xiv, 37–38, 61, 84, 94
Freeman, R. Edward, 26
Friedman, Milton: and corporate responses to Russian invasion of Ukraine, 65; Friedman doctrine, 21–26; and Icahn, Carl 53; and shift toward stakeholder perspective, 28, 29; and Ramaswamy, Vivek, 51

Galloway, Scott, 101–2
Gallup, 31–32
Gartner, 93
General Dynamics Information Technology, 83
General Electric (GE): and establishment of the Business Roundtable, 25; and establishment of Conference Board, 21; and importance of addressing public interest in late 1960s, 22; Immelt, Jeffrey, 5; Wilson, Ian H., 107; Welch, Jack, 24
General Motors (GM), 4, 15
Generation X (Gen X), 19, 24, 28
Generation Z (Gen Z): attitudes on CEOs speaking out, 9, 19; differences with older Americans, 28, 75, 110
Geneva Conventions, 67
Georgia: retaliation against Delta Airlines for canceling NRA passenger discount, 46, 61; voting rights law, 11, 16, 37–39, 83–85
Gilliland, Amy, 83
Glasgow Financial Alliance for Net Zero (GFANZ), 42, 51, 95
GLG, 12–13, 91
Global Reporting Initiative, 97
Global Strategy Group, 64
Glock, 7
Goldman Sachs, 27, 44
Google, 28, 89
Google Scholar, xii
Goya, 103
Groundswell, 89
gun violence: corporate statements about ending, 29, 43; and Dick's Sporting Goods, 88; and issues addressed by CEOs, ix, 6
greenhushing, 44

Harvard Business Review, x
Harvard Law School, 29

Hegar, Glenn, 51–52
Hispanic. See Latino
Hobby Lobby, 34–35
HP, 38
human rights: and corporate inconsistencies, 105; and European Union, 25; and issues addressed by CEOs, 88, 100, 109; public concerns about corporate spin, 19; and public opinion about corporate statements, 17
Human Rights Campaign, 62-63

IBM (International Business Machines): and domestic partner benefits in 1990s, 28; and Fortune 500 in 1970, 22; Krishna, Arvind, 88, 91; and World War II, 86; Watson, Thomas, Jr., 20–21, 31
Icahn, Carl, 53
Iger, Bob, 62–64
Immelt, Jeffrey, 5
immigration: and CEO priorities,13; and CEO responses to Trump administration policy, 80–81, 85; public opinion about 33
Indiana, 36, 52, 99, 108
Intel, 37
investors: accountability to, xv, 56; CEOs addressing, ix, 94, 100, 104; and Bergh, Chip, 29; and climate change, 7, 42–43, 95; and Corbat, Michael, 46; differences between domestic and foreign, xii; Fink, Larry, 2020 letter to CEOs, 3,5, 52; and Friedman, Milton, 23; and Icahn, Carl, 53; listening to, xiv, 73–74; opinions about CEO stances, 18–19; and other stakeholders 4, 82, 110; and Welch, Jack, 24;
IPG Health, 10, 14, 18, 77

Jackson Hole, Wyoming, 35
Jackson Hole Mountain Resort, 35, 89
January 6, 4, 37–39
Japan, 8
Jensen, Michael C., 23
Jeremy's Razors, 34
Jobs, Steve, 80–81
Johnson & Johnson, xiii
Jones, Reginald, 24, 25
Jordan, Jim, 95

ABOUT THE AUTHOR

Matthew Kohut is the coauthor, with Edward J. Hoffman and Laurence Prusak, of *The Smart Mission: NASA's Lessons for Managing Knowledge, People, and Projects* (MIT Press, 2022), which earned the bronze in the business intelligence/innovation category of the 2023 Axiom Awards; and the coauthor, with John Neffinger, of *Compelling People: The Hidden Qualities That Make Us Influential* (Hudson Street Books, 2013), which Amazon named one of the best business books of 2013. As the managing partner of KNP Communications, Kohut has prepared CEOs, elected officials, and public figures for events from live television appearances to TED Talks. He has taught at George Washington University and held a fellowship at Bennington College's Center for the Advancement of Public Action. His writing has appeared in publications ranging from the *Harvard Business Review* to *Newsweek*. He holds a master's degree from Harvard University and a bachelor's degree from Johns Hopkins University.